The Entire Universe

A Poetry Collection

by

Eric Nixon

Cover image and design by Eric Nixon.

© 2014 by Eric Nixon

ISBN-13: 978-0615964669
ISBN-10: 0615964664

Published by Chixon Ink Press in Portland, Oregon.
EricNixonAuthor@gmail.com
EricNixon.net

DEDICATION

This collection is dedicated to my mother-in-law, Janis McWayne, who provided the creative environment in which most of this collection was written.

Thank you!

AUTHOR'S FOREWARD

2013 was an interesting year for me in many ways. Did it go the way I planned? No, not really. Did I get what I wanted? Here and there, yes. Basically, it was a transitional year for me and I feel that is reflected in my writings.

This collection of 265 poems was written between January 1 and December 31, 2013 and, in a way, acts as my own personal diary. I gave up trying to keep an actual diary years ago, but if you do 265 of anything over a single year, a diary of sorts is what it becomes by default. Happiness, joy, frustration, anger, simple observations, hugely deep thoughts, spirituality, and enlightenment are all contained within this year's volume. In 2013 I really learned a lot about myself as a person and as a spiritual being, and I think that comes across in my writings. Everything from minute observations to profound revelations can be found in these pages and I'm glad you're here and can spend a few hours with me on my own journey of self-discovery. Hopefully it'll have an impact on you as well.

Thank you for reading. You just being here hugely motivates me to continue in my poetic pursuit.

Do good work,
Eric

TABLE OF CONTENTS

JANUARY

I Am The Wine You Are The Bananas

In a church
For a wedding
Listening to
The pastor rambling
My eyes bored
And start wandering
Until they land upon
The arch spanning
Above the alter
Up to the ceiling
I see the eight words
And am not believing
So over and over
Reading and attributing
It to the difficult font
Causing the words to
Seem like they're saying
"I am the wine
 you are the bananas"
Making this church
A lot more interesting
Than it was a minute ago

January 1, 2013
Benson, Vermont

Yesterday I went to my cousin's wedding at St. Charles church in Pittsfield, Massachusetts. I've been there a few times before for family funerals. It's a beautiful church but each time I couldn't help but stare up at the words on the huge arch above the alter area, which seriously look like it says, "I am the wine you are the bananas." I think it's the odd, rounded font that makes letters like A, E, U, W, etc., nearly indistinguishable from each other. The difficulty with a font like that is that it could leave the reader slightly confused as to the message they were trying to convey.

To A Man Named Jim Barbour

Half a year ago, we cleared out the garage
Used to be my wife's grandfather's shop
Full of tractor parts, bits of metal, and stuff
When we came across a very heavy old anvil
A quick Google search showed us the history
Lying under the thick layer of dirty dusty
A man in the city of Birmingham set up shop
And worked hard in the mid-1800s
Building his Hill-branded anvils.
Fast forward to the 1990s
To a book called *Anvils in America*
Where the author attested to the rarity
We now found ourselves in possession of
Saying he had only personally seen
Only three of Hills' work in the country.
We, with no need for smithing,
Put it up for sale on Craigslist.
Amid the countless spam
Came a somewhat snarky email
From a man named Jim Barbour
Saying he's found three
Of this particular type
Just in the past year
And then went on to chide
The 20-year old book
Saying they knew nothing.

The man's email meant nothing
And was promptly disregarded,
Ignored, and went unreplied.

Skip ahead to today
When out of the blue
I get another email
From a man named Jim Barbour
The same know-it-all-aplenty
Who sought to educate me

In November of last year.
This time he said pretty much
The exact same thing
Reworded in a way
That seemed to show
He was unaware
Of his own
Previous contact.

I started to write back
With an equally heaping
Dish of heated snark
But I paused, held off,
And thought better of it
Since it would solve nothing
And serve no purpose at all.

I realized it was preferable
To hold my words and let it drop
Than to get into words with a man
Who dispenses his wisdom
To strangers trying to sell things.

This is the email I wanted to
But instead went unsent
To a man named Jim Barbour:
"Thank you again.
 You said something
 Very similar in November
 And I found it to be
 Just as helpful as before.
 Your comments are productive and enriching
 Not just to me, but the whole of society
 So you can relax and rest easy in knowing
 Your place atop the pinnacle of humanity
 Has been maintained, is still outstanding,
 And remains unchallenged in regards to
 The essential and critical world of anvilry."

JANUARY

January 1, 2013
Benson, Vermont

I had written just the first sentence of that email when I had stopped and decided to do something creative with it rather than get involved in a "discussion" with some guy I don't know about a subject I don't care about.

Retreating

Retreat to step back
Retreat to plan
Retreat to charge ahead
Retreating doesn't mean
What you think it does
Retreating is the process
Where we pause
And prepare to attack

> January 2, 2013
> Hudson, New York

We're on a retreat to plan out our year. It's going quite well.

I'm Just Learning To Live

Words overheard
In the busy noisy
Mexican restaurant:
"I'm just learning to live"
Said a man who's been alive
For just as long as I have
While wearing nice clothes
Not found in any local mall
Playing with the shiny keys
Of his brand new sports car.
Uninterested, I tuned him out
As I didn't care to know more
About the reasons for his words
And instead imagined a newborn
Tiny, bald, and only days old
Saying the exact same thing
With a wise and knowing nod
While wearing a nice onesie
With a cute cartoony cat.
That would make more sense
And would be more acceptable
Within the context of his words
Again proving I prefer the world
In my head to the one outside.

January 2, 2013
Hudson, New York

Casualties Of The Season

I looked up at the bright apartment
Full of life apart from the dark tree
Unlit in the window, biding its time
In the brief awkward stage
Between nightly reverence
And the unceremonious dumping
Due to happen any day now.
It was probably in the process
Of being stripped of its lights
Having its ornaments unhooked
Being undressed and dedecorated.
Soon its identity will be gone
And it'll end up in the landfill
Or tossed in the woods
Like millions of its brethren;
Casualties of the season.

                    January 3, 2013
                    Hudson, New York

Seeing that dark tree in the wide picture window really got me
thinking.

Hudson Is Not Afraid Of Color

Hudson is not afraid of color
Dressing its beautiful architecture
In a striking visual array
Drawing attention to the buildings
And the intricate details
That often go overlooked,
Unappreciated, and unnoticed
In other cities from a similar age

January 4, 2013
Hudson, New York

One of the first things you notice about Hudson is the very colorful
buildings. That, and the fascinating architecture. I don't know if
the building design is just extraordinary in this town or if it's like
this everywhere and I only noticed it because of the color.

Enjoy

In the other room
Of our hotel suite
The iPad burst to life
Completely on its own
Playing "Enjoy" by Bjork
On its never-used iTunes.
I went and turned it off
And we noted how strange
That it started by itself
Especially since we haven't
Listened to music on that device.
A few minutes later
Bjork begins to sing again
With no one near
To press anything.
Once would be dismissible
Twice would be impossible.
Maybe it's a mindful ghost
Residing in this hip hotel
Who cares about hospitality
Providing us with music
And a message of joy.
Or, considering the date
Maybe it's my father
Celebrating his birthday
Telling me to enjoy life
While I'm still in it.

While the music is nice, and the intentions
Behind the playing might be as well
Any way this situation is looked upon
Is, well, still a bit creepy.

> January 4, 2013
> Hudson, New York

This actually happened and freaked us out a little bit. When we got the iPad, I loaded a bunch of songs on it, but we listen to music on our iPods or our iPhones. Honestly, we've never used the iPad for music before, which is why this was more than weird.

Everything He Wants

At a Dunkin Donuts
Sitting two tables down
From an angry white man
Wearing checkered fleece
White hair, back and slicked
Complaining about everything
Saying how it figures
All the bad stuff happens
Only to him, all the time
Proving without a doubt
How he is quite adept
With the Law of Attraction
Attracting everything he wants
Which is nothing but negativity

January 4, 2013
Kinderhook, New York

Not only was this guy so negative, but he was being all showy and loud about it, like he was trying to be braggy about it.

Sky Up, Ice Down

Up, up, far up above
Sits the bluest of skies
Deeper than an ocean
Prettier than a sapphire
Laced with puffy lines
Like a planely-made
Aeronautical embellishment

Up, just a few feet above
Sits a row of jagged ice
Glittering like sticks of diamonds
Icicling, looming, pointing downward
With pretty malevolent intentions
The situation quickly diffused
With a reach, a snap, and a drop

Down, down, to the ground
The sharp point hits and breaks
Shattering like glass on the slick
Solid puddle layering around
Where the drippings of the ice
Fell and froze into a reflecting sheet
Mirroring the magnificent blue sky

January 6, 2013
Benson, Vermont

The other day I took a neat picture. The top half was an insanely
blue sky threaded with a contrail. The bottom half was the edge of
the lower roof and looked like the toothy maw of some ice
monster. I like it when one artistic outlet (in this case,
photography) inspires another (poetry).

Failure Portion

You successfully navigated
Your youth years
And transitioned well
Into and through college
Your 20s were
So very fantastic
So full of promise
A well-paying job
In a solid career
Advancing the ladder
With steady regularity
Married to your spouse
Everything was looking up
Until…
Noises, bumps, scrapes
Small at first but growing
In size, scope, and regularity
Your late 20s felt different
Dulled, tinged, clouded
And the thrill once felt had faded
Like a faint childhood memory.

Jittery, roughly, drearily
You coasted into your mid-30s
Divorce number one done
Single parent working
Locked in a joyless job
Chipping away at the towering
Impossibly high glacier
Of backlogged debt
The bills endlessly hungry
Quickly devouring the brief
Bi-weekly plus in the account
Bringing back to near zero
Making you look longingly
At the days so many years ago
And wonder what happened

Wonder how you got from
Point A to point Z
With B seeming like
A dream-like impossibility
So far from where you
Were supposed to go
So far from where you
Were supposed to be
Not here, not stuck
Not anything like this
When the anti-depressants
Do nothing to protect
Do nothing to mute
The approaching whistle
Of the oncoming
Mid-life express train
Arriving way too early
Not to take you
But to slam you
Where you stand
Leaving you crushed,
Dazed, and stranded
In the failure portion
Of your life.

January 7, 2013
Benson, Vermont

So many people these days started out their lives with seemingly
unlimited potential and success that just click, click, clicked into
place. Then, fifteen to twenty years later, they're divorced,
somehow went from a great job to a crappy low-paying one, and
buried in a mountain of debt. Sadly, this seems to be the new norm.

Pretty Full Plate

Pretty full plate
More like a buffet
Where focusing
On just one thing
Is so hard to do
Due to distraction
Always there, vying
For your attention

January 7, 2013
Benson, Vermont

The Entire Universe

Most can never get to the point
Where they shake up the dust
And shift the entire universe
Because they are much too busy
Being disturbed by the stirring
Of things within their own space

> January 7, 2013
> Benson, Vermont

I just read the T.S. Eliot line, "Do I dare disturb the universe," on a design blog that makes neat frameable art with quotes from writers (ObviousState.com). I was instantly inspired to write this.

Peachy Sunset

Peachy sunset
Or maybe tangerine
Some sort of fruit
Spread thick on the horizon
Looking up from that point
The color fastly fades
Into a muted white
And changes again
As the eyes continue up
To a pale powder blue
Marred by a passing plane's
Severely stark white slice
Contrail comet

January 8, 2013
Benson, Vermont

A neat sunset I saw yesterday.

Entrenched

Those who are in it
So deeply
Welcome the new blood
With disdain and scorn
For the terrible crime
Of having discovered
A passing interest in it
Well after they did.
Despite being deeply entrenched
They look down on everyone
With their noses held high
Effectively ensuring
They see nothing
But their own
Very inflated
Importance
And
Self-worth

January 8, 2013
Benson, Vermont

I think everyone's met this kind of person, whether it be at a new job, or a club, or social group, or whatever. I usually come across people like this in an online game I play.

The Receding White

The heat goes up
The depth recedes
The receding white
The revealing retreat

> January 9, 2013
> Benson, Vermont

The temperature is in the 40s (Fahrenheit) today and the snow level has been decreasing steadily.

Listening To A Song

Listening to a song
That grabs me forcefully
And takes me strongly, quickly
To a region I've never been,
To a specific house I've never seen
Where I see myself years from now
Standing in a huge living room
Feeling the warmth of the fireplace
Walking over to the window
Holding a glass of wine
Looking out the floor-to-ceiling
Viewing the well-past-sunset
Darkening navy of night
Settling in over the Pacific
And forces me to feel
Something I've never felt
A potent mix of nostalgia,
Longing, regret, loneliness,
Success, accomplishment,
Comfort, and contentment.
So many conflicting emotions
All living in harmony
While I'm steeped in serenity
Blissful and happy despite it all.

January 12, 2013
Benson, Vermont

I don't know why, but every single time I listen to David Gray's "Please Forgive Me," my mind gets taken away to a very real setting: it's sometime in the future and I'm maybe in my early 50s or so. I'm in a super-modern house standing in a big living room that's open to the equally big kitchen behind me. In front of me is a very large fireplace, which is giving off most of the light. I feel the warmth coming from it. I turn to my left and walk over to the floor-to-ceiling windows that provide an amazing view of the

Pacific Ocean down below. I actually can't really see it because it's about 90% dark and I can just make out a smudge of navy blue on the horizon left over from the sunset an hour before. I sip from my glass of wine and say nothing as I appreciate the darkened view. Within me is an odd mixture of emotions, but despite the negative ones of sadness and regret, a reassuring wave of comfort is there letting me know everything's ok. I feel and see all of this in my mind every time I listen to this song. It's crazy powerful.

The Most Amazing And Least Constructive

The most amazing and productive tool
Ever in the grand story of humanity
Holds an equally negative title
As the least constructive contrivance
Ever in the history of civilization

Congratulations, Internet!

> January 12, 2013
> Benson, Vermont

There are days when I'm just astounded at how much the Internet has changed humanity for the better…and other days when it is the biggest distractor ever.

As If Painted By God Himself

Breathtaking sunset,
A photo opportunity
Catching my sharp eye
Horizon-wide before me
As if painted by God Himself
(Award-worthy for sure)
I start to plan to capture
The fleeting perfection
But the logistics defied me
I'm here inside, and there's
Too much in the way:
A barn, scraggly trees,
And two feet of snow
Separating me from
The perfect shot
There, it's right there,
The cloud layers
With their fiery undersides
Hanging under,
Burning beneath,
Ice gray tops
Layering atop each other
Shaping the exquisite view
Each moment the sight grew slighter
Slightly fading
Color draining
Ever ebbing
Quickly diminishing
Until it was extinguished
By the conspiring couple
Of our planet's rotation
And time.
With that, the beauty was gone.

Looking at the lingering wisps
I'm one part sad
I didn't get the picture

JANUARY

And five parts glad
The universe had me
In the right place
At the right time
To have been able
To not just witness
But experience
And appreciate it.

January 12, 2013
Benson, Vermont

This happened the other day.

The Words We Use

The words we use
Can be used
To lift people up
Or knock them down.
Speak conscientiously
For they are weighted
With power and meaning
And should never be
Casually or lightly thrown.

> January 13, 2013
> Benson, Vermont

This came about from a combination of listening to the public radio show *On Being*, and "What Difference Does It Make" by The Smiths.

Fonty

Writing something and I want to make it look pretty.
Spending entirely too long choosing just the right font.
Hours gone considering serifs, something, and widths,
Meanwhile the words involved have lost all meaning.
I'm going fonty-font crazy from too many choices.

January 13, 2013
Benson, Vermont

Ha! I almost typed "Benson, Vermonty."

Making A Mockery Of The Process

When someone voices an opinion
The disagreeable types are often
The first to demand they shut up
With threats, intimidation, and force
Making a mockery of the process
Regarding debate on the Constitution
Being unaware of the hefty irony
That looms and shadows all they do

January 13, 2013
Benson, Vermont

Outspiration

Although similar, outspiration
Is a whole lot like inspiration
Except it happens outdoors

January 13, 2013
Benson, Vermont

Kind of like how meteors and asteroids are the same thing except
for where they happen to be located.

Poet's Seat

Like a book by its cover
I judged a place by its name
And was left unimpressed
Reflecting on my way home
Poet's Seat should be relocated
A few mountains down
Up high atop Sugarloaf
Which has an inspiring view
More worthy of the name
And the image it creates

January 13, 2013
Benson, Vermont

While I'm sure Frederick Goddard Tuckerman thought the view from the Poet's Seat overlook in Greenfield, Massachusetts was pretty nifty, I found it to be hardly inspiring. The tower there is pretty cool, though.

If you want a truly inspiring view, go to Sugarloaf in South Deerfield, Massachusetts. That's the perfect place to see all of the Pioneer Valley and the Connecticut River in mid-curve.

Physics-Defying Ice Sheet

For the past few days
I've watched with
Increased fascination
As the ice on a low roof
Crept out over the edge
Just a little bit at first
But now it's absurd
Hanging a foot and a half
Over the threshold
With only six inches of it
Resting on the roof which
Seems to be impossible.
I should knock it down
So it doesn't fall on me
But I want to see how
Nature resolves this
Physics-defying ice sheet.
I'm secretly hoping
It keeps on sliding
Out and over the edge
And keeps on going -
Floating off into the night.
The reality is I'll be the one
Cleaning it off the walk
First thing in the morning.

January 13, 2013
Benson, Vermont

It's been unseasonably warm lately (in the 50s – Fahrenheit) and all of the snow is melting. As a result, all of the ice on the roof is slowly sliding off. It's getting comical how much of this ice sheet is hanging off compared to the little bit that's actually on the roof.

Scenes From A Future Here

A mid-January day rightly confused
With bright sun, warm weather,
And a mostly avocado grass ocean
Sporadicked with archipelagic snow.
The rich green smell of damp earth
Came whispering in on the warm wind
Commanding an extra deep breath,
A welcoming drink of what's to come
Like the hard diamond needle
Skipping the seasonal groove
And playing a wrong-song snippet
Of scenes from a future here
Past the winter, in two month's time.

January 14, 2013
Benson, Vermont

Amid The Thunderous Din

A desire waits for impulse – the impulse waits for opportunity
A neuron fired, deep in the brain, starting the chain of events
Leading to the junctious meeting of chemicals and the physical
The place where thoughts become actions
Among the backdropping heartbeat quickening
Faster, at first guiding, before soon taking over,
Running things, fingers tracing, touching, causing actions
Previously unconsidered, undared in the deepest dreams,
Unknown anywhere but the unthought-of world where
The mind shuts down, unneeded and subservient to the senses
Drawn together by magnetism, gravity, and repeating rhythm
Operating on powerful feelings, breathily responding to nuance –
Cycling and repeating like a whirlpool of the sensory
Spinning faster and tighter until all is consumed amid the
thunderous din

January 14, 2013
Benson, Vermont

The first line has been sitting in Line Ideas for a few months now.
In fact, I found it near the long-forgotten depthly bottom of that
document. Over the past week or so I've been tinkering with this
and finished it this morning.

Coin On Cardboard

Second in line at the convenience store
The first was being waited on
And knows the clerk by name
Not as friends, but in a professional way
He asked for "the usual"
As he tossed a crumpled used lottery ticket
Over the counter and into a wastebasket.

After goods and money were exchanged
He turned away to one side
As if steeped within
A deeply private moment
With one hand furiously rubbing
Coin on cardboard
Faster, as if the extra speed and power
Would lead him, somehow, to victory.
I could almost feel
The fleeting hope evaporate from
His rote motion
As he gradually slowed
And his dream-like redemption
Faded with the realization
That, yet again, he wasn't a winner.
Reacting with a deep sigh
And the instinctual crumple
Conditioned from his two-dollar habit
He got back in line
Opened his wallet
Removed two singles
And was ready to try again.

January 15, 2013
Benson, Vermont

What I saw yesterday in Fair Haven.

Beauty Inherent (A Choose-A-Better-Ending Poem)

Beauty inherent
Is rarely apparent
To those who are not
A spouse or a parent
But those who can see
The deep inner beauty
Will be rewarded
With a love most sturdy*

>   January 15, 2013
>   Benson, Vermont

*Let's have some fun with that poem up there! Replace the last line with your favorite from the following list:

Buying a new shoe tree
Being kinda smoochy
With a furry yeti
With a coat most tweedy
With a sheep so wooly
With a super zombie
With a cup of coffee
With a pint of whiskey
Wearing pants so baggy
Dating that guy, Andy
Feeling somewhat stabby
Feeling kinda sorry
Feeling kinda spicy
Feeling kinda gassy
Feeling sore and achy
Covered in bad acne
Screaming like a banshee
Dressing up so fancy
Driving a new taxi
Drinking a lot of tea
Eating some shrimp scampi

Getting rudely rutty
Jumping from a belfry
Falling in a quarry
Demanding a freebie
Drinking a whole Pepsi
Going to the deli
Going to an orgy
Making a new baby
Making lots of cookies
Eating a nice pastry
Eating really healthy
Eating some hot chili
Wearing a new nighty
With a love most lovely
Screaming really loudly
Watching I Love Lucy
Going to the laundry
Going to Friendly's
Dating a new hussy
Dating a new furry
Dating a drunk druggie
Leaving in a hurry
Sailing in a dinghy
Swimming to a buoy
Petting a cute doxie

Curiosity Shoppe

A small New Englandy village
With a one-block downtown
And in the center of it all
Is a tiny curiosity shoppe
(Yes, with the extra P and E)
Specializing in things like
Trinkets, souvenirs,
Knickknacks, ornaments,
And other crap no one needs.
It's enough to make
The casual observer
Curious as to how
This odd shoppe
Can possibly
Remain open
In these Internetal days
And these financial times.

                    January 16, 2013
                    Benson, Vermont

Seriously? In a non-touristy town, how does a "curiosity shoppe"
remain in business? I would think that people are a lot tighter with
their discretionary funds and buying a country cutesy sign that says
"butter" would not be high on their list of priorities. Plus, if
someone did want something like that, I would assume they'd find
it online before just happening across it in some shop in a tiny
town. It just makes me curious, which, in turn, perpetuates the
place.

A Succinctly Concise Overview Of An Unhealthy Relationship

Attraction
Fascination
Passion
Obsession
Friction
Repulsion
(Immediately repeat
 With a new person)

> January 16, 2013
> Benson, Vermont

Some song that came up on my playlist a little while ago had the word "attraction" in it. For some reason I took the short crazy route.

On The Eighteenth (Not The Nineteenth)

Every year I'm wrong
Again and again and again
I always think my cousin's birthday
Is on the nineteenth
But it's not
It's on the eighteenth
And every year I'm caught off-guard
A day earlier than I expect
I'm not really sure why
I continue to believe this
When my iCal and Facebook
Always try to correct me
To remember the right date
So happy birthday to Patrick
Who turns a year older today
On the eighteenth
(Not the nineteenth)
Of January

January 18, 2013
Benson, Vermont

It would be a lot easier if he could change his birthday to match
what I think it is.

A Drip Thought Lost

There are times when the words I write
Feel more formidable than an earthquake
In their ability to move and resonate
There are other times when the words I write
Feel as ineffective as a quiet word whispered in a hurricane
Like a single pine needle compared to the entirety of Maine.
It all depends on the thoughts that brought them to being:
A supernova idea blasting across light years,
A drip thought lost in an ocean Atlantic;
Both are equally powerful in their own way.
Explosive energy compared to traced nuance,
The sensor depends on that of the reader
And the sensitivity of their emotional radar
As those who can pick it up, the barely there nothingness
Ignored and dismissed by others,
Are treated to a God-like hammer blow to their senses.

> January 18, 2013
> Benson, Vermont

It's all perspective. You could listen to a single drip drop into a
sink full of water recorded in high definition, played back slowly,
and magnified in a stadium-like setting and it would sound like a
bomb going off.

Citymatic View

Thinking back to all the places I've lived
The one that resonates and fits the most
With my younger view of what it means
To be an adult was a year in the high-rise
Four towns north, a hundred feet vertical
With a wide view of Boston before me
Mid-sized city living a five-minute walk
To the subway, putting me in the big city
Feeling like I had made it, I was successful
In having gotten away from my little town
Left that life far behind and moved on up.
My mid-twenties were wide-eyed enough
To be constantly impressed by what I saw
But also smart enough to know this wasn't
My forever place, not by a long shot, no sir.
Still though, I can't help but to occasionally
Reminisce on the setting and want a similar
Situation, just in a vastly different location,
Someplace that will make me feel adultish
With a towering, well-lit, citymatic view
That can inspire me from what I will see
And provide unlimited daily living options.

January 19, 2013
Benson, Vermont

Just thinking aloud to myself (in a structured way – I wanted each line to be as close as possible to the same length) about living locations.

Frownloadable

Typing too quickly
A finger on my left hand
Tapping too far over
Landing right on the F
When my intention was
The D-key to the left
The keystroke error
Changing the concept
Altering the words
I was writing;
Downloadable
Became
Frownloadable
Which, at first,
Caused me to pause
Then, at last,
Caused me to laugh
As I considered
Possible instances
When I've been
Exactly that way.

January 22, 2013
Benson, Vermont

I haven't bothered to Google this because I'm partly afraid it's already a thing/word/phrase and I didn't inadvertently make it up.

Esque

Sort of near
Kind of close
Can and will be
Compared to
A semblance
Of a resemblance while
In the neighborhood
And knowing full well
Its doppelganger is lurking about
With similar intentions,
Still refusing to meet up
And admitting a sameness
But instead choosing to plead:
"Esque"

> January 22, 2013
> Benson, Vermont

Bookmark

Knowing where you are is important
And owing to a simple strip of paper
Picking up from the spot where you left off
Is easy with the bookmark you left behind
Reserving your residence in that world
Saving your place while you paused

January 22, 2013
Benson, Vermont

Tonight I designed a promotional bookmark for Kari's books and it got me thinking about the word "bookmark" and what it does.

Every Picture Is A Porthole

The heartache of time slipped by
Leaving only a frame
Containing the captured square of a moment
Stopping the second
Freezing the light
Holding the youth
That once lived there, right there
Always alongside
Assuming forevermore
Until the dark ravaging of time
Stepped in, and said nevermore.
No matter how wonderful things are
Nothing will ever stay the same
Feelings, people, lives, time
It all changes
It all shifts
It moves and morphs
Rendering those moments
Lost to the present
And the memories
Thick, dense, and overbearing
With the longing for the past
Can never be reclaimed
Can never be relived
But instead are continually replayed
Where every picture is a porthole
Giving a glimpse to the past
As the ship sails on
And going back
Is an impossibility
As every moment
Drags you further away
From that point in time,
Leaving only the
Jarring, jabbing, icepicking, paining ache
Of regret in its wake.

January 23, 2013
Benson, Vermont

I subscribe to a few Tumblr feeds on my Google Reader. One of them posts maybe twenty, or so, pictures a day…usually things like vintage pictures, maps, random people doing random things, coffee, etc. I always find them to be neat glimpses into the world. Tonight, one of these pictures stopped me dead in my tracks and I immediately was inspired…well, that's not the right word, maybe *impulsed* to write a poem based on this photo. Since I don't know who it belongs to, I won't re-print it but I'll try to describe it (to see it for yourself, go to emtc.tumblr.com/post/41291293721):

In a square photo is a face-on shot of a woman, in her early-to-mid 20s, about to drink a coffee at night. You see her from the chest up. She's wearing a 70s-ish tan coat with a wide pointy, wooly sheepskin collar. Her hair is best described as an overgrown pixie; short and brown but starting to get a little unruly and tousled. She is holding a double-cupped paper coffee cup, which is up at chin-level. Her full lips are pursed as if she was caught in the process of bringing this cup to her mouth. It is nighttime but she is somewhere where there is a bright light source lighting her left side, casting shadows over the right side of her face and shoulder. In the blurry background there are three men. A black man wearing a t-shirt is drinking a coffee over her left shoulder. Over her right shoulder, in the moderate distance, are two very blurry men wearing jeans, fall jackets, and are wearing hats; one yellow, one green.

I think what caught my eye and my emotions so deeply with this photo was that, on the surface, it's just a random moment in time featuring a random woman, but the person who took this photo probably has a deep emotional connection. Maybe the woman is a current, or past, love, and maybe this photo was taken at a happy random moment five, ten, fifteen, twenty years ago. That's the thing - this photo seems timeless. It could have been taken at any point in the past 30 years. If it was taken recently, to the taker, it probably doesn't hold much sway…but if it was taken decades ago during a long-ago exhausted youth, this picture probably means the world to them.

Doublecupped

Trying to pick up but can't –
The paper cup's too hot
For the hand to hold.
No sleeves that can be seen;
No time to let it cool down.
The answer: doublecupped.

January 24, 2013
Benson, Vermont

I think this is wasteful, but then again, I don't drink coffee.

Unstable

Much like a horse barn
Being bossed around
And not being used
For its original intention
The unstable has a way
With words, with moods
Irrational and debilitating
And ends up leaving
The horse out in the cold
Feeling lonely and confused

January 25, 2013
Benson, Vermont

Look But Cannot Touch

Pinpoints of light
Seemingly randomly
Created, placed, and hung
In the nighttime dome
So high, so far above
Where we can look
But cannot touch.
Despite the advent
Of space-based telescopes
Which allow us to see
The stars surrounding
With stunning quality
And every year
The pictures from space
Only get better
As we see further
And it all comes closer,
Closer in view,
But even though
The quality improves
Neither you nor I
Will ever get to go
Will ever get to see
A planet or a star
Up close for real
Other than our own.

January 26, 2013
Benson, Vermont

One of the downsides to having access to amazing space
photography is the nagging knowing that we won't ever get to go
to these places in our lifetime.

Terms Of Service

Sixty-five pages
Purposely boring
Written in legalese
Effectively ensuring
You'll never skim it
Just click without
Reading the contents
Accept and forget it
That's what they want
To give you too much
To process, to handle,
Hoping you'll be passive,
Accepting, and unknowing
Of the terms of service

January 26, 2013
Benson, Vermont

The last time I updated iTunes I was struck with how crazy-insane their terms of service are. I don't know if it was sixty-five pages, but it was close. The thing is, the average person will never ever read it, especially when there's a handy "Click and accept" button that lets you skip the painful document.

When The Numbers Dip Drop

Zero tumbling
To negative ten
(Maybe more)
Fahrenheit,
Much more if you count
The efforts made
By the wind
Chiply, sharply
Cutting through
Like an ice scythe
Twenty, thirty…
Never mind,
It makes no difference
Since it's all the same
When the numbers dip drop
Into an unhelpful state
Making risking going outside
A completely avoidable venture

> January 26, 2013
> Benson, Vermont

It has been quite cold for the past week, with temps in the negative numbers (F) every day and night.

There Is No Conflict

Despite the common belief
There is no conflict
Between the business
And creative minds,
As those who can't make a go of it
Often reiterate.
To infer there is a division
Is to deny the possibilities,
Gainings, and rewards
That can be gotten
From the fruitful
Marriage of the two.
Assume that success
Is entirely boundless
And dependent not on
Anything else but
Your positive mindset.

January 27, 2013
Benson, Vermont

When you work with, or know a lot of creatives, you hear the same excuse over and over again – "I can't do the business side of things because I'm a creative person!" Anyone who thinks that is just limiting themselves. Anybody can do anything. There was a point in every expert's life where they knew nothing about their topic of expertise.

To Action

A chord
A note
A pause
A beat
In the proper proportions
Inspired by sensation
Stirred by source
Measured in meter
Can churn the deepest
Emotions
Can float the powerful
Feelings
Can cause such primal
Longings
Moving those who hear
To action
In whatever form
That may be

January 27, 2013
Benson, Vermont

I find a gigantic amount of inspiration and (especially) motivation from music. I'm like an emotional dowsing rod – if I have music playing that I feel is in tune with a certain emotion, I lock onto that and can write as if I had a pen filled ink made of that feeling. Music is powerful.

Terrible Territory

Open thoughts and remarks
In a closed-minded place
Inspire and spark action
Among those who react
With violent infliction
Instead of pausing to think
As the reasonable would
But choose to lash out
Escalating the situation
Into terrible territory
From which society
Can never recover

January 29, 2013
Benson, Vermont

While not written about any one specific event, it's unfortunate that the world seems to have entirely more than its fair share of those who lack the emotional wherewithal to clarify their feelings through speech and thoughtful debate and instead choose to express themselves with violence.

I Feel Like A Gardener

Today I feel like a gardener
The groundskeeper of verse
As I read through the lines
Watering and adding to some
Pruning and trimming others
Repotting those who need a transplant
And tossing ones that died long ago
Basically just doing maintenance
On all the greenery
In my poetic greenhouse
Coaching the ugly
Coaxing the beauty
Making them pretty
Prepping them for the day
A whole year away
When I have my garden sale
And send them off to new homes
To emotionally ensnare,
Inspire, and ensmile
The lives of their new owners

January 29, 2013
Benson, Vermont

While going through my Line Ideas document and tweaking my
slowly growing collection of not-quite-ready poetry lines, this idea
popped into my head.

The Entire Universe

FEBRUARY

Hangry

Hungry
Plus some
Angry
Equals
Hangry

February 1, 2013
South Deerfield, Massachusetts

I'm counting my calorie intake with an app and I'm equally
appalled and stunned at how many calories yummy things are.

Little Sheep

Little sheep
Are quiet
Sitting silent
Yet telling
Showing me
The shortcut
Quickly taken
Making this
Hotel bed
I'm lying in
Apparently
Discoveredly
Dirty

February 2, 2013
South Deerfield, Massachusetts

My mom's birthday is this coming week so we went down to Massachusetts to spend a couple of days with her. When Kari and I got in bed at the hotel last night I saw several really long hairs at the head of the bed. I shrugged whatever and dropped them on the floor. As I pulled back the sheet I saw a whole flock of little curly black "sheep"*. There were too many to brush off and it was too late so we slept on top of the sheet where it was debris free. It appears that whoever cleaned the room just re-made the bed without changing the sheets.

*When I first started in my career as a hotel manager, I got a call from an irate guest who said there was a lot of pubic hair all over the toilet of the room she just checked into. Our funny Middle-Eastern houseman went up to the room. A few minutes later he came back and reported, "Sheep. Baa! Sheep everywhere. Little sheep all over toilet. Baa! I clean, they drown, it's good. No more sheep."

Teetering On The Edge

The apex of the moment
When the realization
Pauses at the peak
As the dawning thoughts
Rush in as gravity kicks on
Stop it, freeze it solid,
Before the car
Runs out of control
Blurring blindingly
Down the tracks,
Before the thoughts
Get ahead of themselves
Racing ragingly
Across the lives,
Because once you let it go
And let inertia take over
Stretching a ruinous moment
Across a lifetime of regret,
You can never return
To this moment of clarity
Right here, where you're
Teetering on the edge
Between sanity
And a lack thereof
So use this fraction of a second
And choose wisely
Because all future seconds
Hinge on what you do
Right
Now

> February 2, 2013
> Benson, Vermont

Just as I was finishing the poem "Little Sheep" the phrase "the apex of the moment" appeared in my mind and I just ran with it.

These Boxes Have A Gravity

Thinking too far way up there
In the lofty attic of my mind
Where I rarely spend time
Among the dusty recesses
And the cluttered boxes
The more occasions I'm
Up here living in the past
The more I'd rather be
Down there in the yard
Feeling the sunny day,
Living in the moment,
And enjoying the present
But still these boxes
Have a gravity all their own
Strongly pulling me back.
I used to not resist so much
But lately, it's been easier
As nothing changes up here
It's the same old everything
Whereas down there, outside
It's all-new, every moment,
Every thought, every second
Holds a new experience for me
Which I find more appealing
Than unchanging reruns
Dimmed with time
And covered in dust

February 4, 2013
Benson, Vermont

I realized how terrible it is to waste the present thinking about the past.

Don't Shake The Etch-A-Sketch

Don't shake the Etch-A-Sketch
You'll wipe out my work
All of the knob-fiddling
And delicate fine-tuning
Will be lost to your meddling
Preserve my creation intact
Twist, turn, keep it going
Despite us both knowing
Too much effort is being
Expended in making
This blocky, ugly,
Wholly awful rendering

February 4, 2013
Benson, Vermont

I had written a poem ten years ago with the same title. It was a really awful attempt at writing a deep-meaning, multi-layered political poem. I ended up deleting the poem, but I was intrigued with the title, so I kept it in Line Ideas. This version is more honest.

Watering A Dead Plant

Watering a dead plant
Going through the motions
Not noticing, not caring
Indifference coolly burning
While still faithfully repeating
The job with a mind elsewhere
Active, alive, and so far away
Focused on a plantless future
Where a passionate living,
Full of details and caring,
Is the joyous new normal

February 4, 2013
Benson, Vermont

At one hotel I worked at, we had a whole bunch of mums that
needed to be watered every night. It was the job of the overnight
employee to water them…something he very rarely did because
every morning I would come in and find the plants near death. For
him it was just a job (one he really didn't give a hoot about), and
he had much bigger plans, which I totally sympathize with and
could relate to. I imagine that this poem is what it would have been
like to peek into his head.

Become My Night

All at once
I want to listen to everything
Every song I own
To feel the words, the music
Envelop me, become my night
Guide my thoughts
Thousands of ideas
Hundreds of voices
All of it now
Not enough time
For it all to fit
But watch me try

February 8, 2013
Benson, Vermont

All of a sudden, I have a real craving to listen to a whole bunch of music. So many different songs and bands, all vying to be played next.

There Comes A Point

There comes a point
In every successful life
When they eschew
The supposed assumptions
Of their graduating class
(Unseen for many years
 But still firmly in mind)
And live according
To their own dictates
Not caring what anyone,
Lest of all those who knew, think
And press on with their own lives
Fully free of worry,
Completely carefree,
And most of all, happy

February 8, 2013
Benson, Vermont

Lately I've been thinking a lot about my image. Mostly, I've thought about what if someone I knew from high school saw my website and I got to wondering what they would think. Well, not so much "wondered," but instead "worried." After a few days of giving this way too much thought, I came to this important conclusion: who cares. Seriously. There are a ton more important things to be focused on than what the two-decade-in-the-past versions of people I used to know think about me now. With that realization, I felt a whole lot freer and was able to move on.

Stolen Seconds

Looking through the menu
Wondering quietly to myself
While trying to figure out
What can I buy with the stolen seconds
Squirreled away over the course of my life
So much I've always wanted
So much I can now have
Faced with the problem
Of pacing my spending
Fitting everything in the space
I have left from now to the end

> February 12, 2013
> Benson, Vermont

I woke up at 4:30 this morning with the phrase, "What can I buy with the stolen seconds," forefront in my mind. I typed it into the notepad on my phone and as I started to drift off to sleep I had more ideas…but I forgot them because I didn't write them down. Note to self: don't believe me when I tell myself, "Don't worry. I don't need to write it down, I'll remember this," because I totally won't.

A Muted Vibrancy

Life, a touch changed
Dulled by the days
Stricken by malaise
Suffered into the shape
Of a muted vibrancy
Deeply ensconced
Amidst faded senses
To that mellow place
Barely noticed where
Exclamation points
Dusty with unused
Obliviousness
Languish among
The lower peaks,
Mellower ebbs,
Subdued sensations,
Heightened indifference,
And emotional surrender
Rarely straying
From the center,
The middle of things,
The summation of which
Will result in
Something of a
Hastened vacancy
If enough strength
And determination
Can be mustered
To overcome
The lackluster weight
Pressing all sides,
Pushing inward

February 12, 2013
Benson, Vermont

Not what I'm feeling but I came up with the title phrase a few days ago and, with inspiration from some mellow songs, wrote the rest.

Slow Turn Out Of The Driveway

The slow turn out of the driveway
Seen from the second floor
Where it seemed as if the car
Was doubly hampered by gravity
Or a mellow regretful lingering
As the beams swept to the side
Slowly before straightening
As the vehicle crept along
With the driver's eyes
Not on the cold road, but stuck
On the lively living room lights
Wishing the events of the evening
Had transpired differently,
Had resulted in anything,
But driving home alone

February 15, 2013
Benson, Vermont

I watched as my mother-in-law's boyfriend's son's car (that is a lot
of possessive cases!) left the driveway. He came over for dinner;
no biggie. Seeing the car turning got me thinking what if it was a
different situation where one person was visiting someone they
liked and things didn't go as hoped or planned.

A Mote Of Nothingness

A bit of rock
A mote of nothingness
Edged too close
And was pulled in
Into a collision,
A fiery embrace,
With a pale blue dot -
Heated by the layers
Arcing across the sky
Like a firedot lancing
As brightly as a star falling
Causing much commotion
And frenzied speculation
Among the land-bound dwellers

February 15, 2013
Benson, Vermont

I'm acutely aware of, and interested in, all things space-related.
When I first saw the Tweets this morning about the meteor in
Russia, I got all kinds of excited. And wow, those videos of it
blazing through the sky – so amazing!

Pausal Quit

Suddenly abruptly stopping
Caused by the dawning
That it's just not worth it
Resulting in a pausal quit
Ending it all right then and there

February 16, 2013
Benson, Vermont

Drained And Done

My eyelids weighty with the weariness
My mouth can't stop the silent screaming
As yawns keep forcing their way out
With my chin planted and palm-held
I slow-blink back the fatigue,
Eye up to the corner clock
And resign myself to the fact
That this day is drained and done

February 16, 2013
Benson, Vermont

Goodnight.

Liquid Addiction

Every morning I push the button
Sending hot water draining through
The ground grains down
Black hot dripping, pooling, pouring
Into the insulated carafe –
Every morning but today
When something went wrong
And nothing happened
Angering those who rely on it
By disrupting their rote routine
And starving their liquid addiction

February 19, 2013
Benson, Vermont

The coffee maker in the house broke and sent Kari and her mom into a tizzy.

Dragshund

Crazy dream where I was
Trapped
In some school's gymnasium
Afraid
Of the looming monster outside
Warned
Others not to go out there
Watched
As a shadow swooped down
Cringed
When the long jaw aimed and
Chomped
The stupidly brave fellow who
Screamed
Loudly, flailed about and was
Swallowed
By the fearsome, thirty-foot long
Winged
Beast that flapped, sailed, and
Wound
Itself around a nearby tree,
Licked
It's lips hungrily while it
Wagged
And whapped its dappled tail as the
Dragshund,
Half dragon, half dachshund,
Waited
Excitedly for another fleshy treat

February 19, 2013
Benson, Vermont

And when I woke up, there were two of them surrounding me! But
they were miniature and didn't have wings...or dragon parts.

Under The Stars

Looking up
Dots, points, twinkles
So close but just out of reach
I want to take one home
To brighten my room
With heavenly light
I could do it –
I have a ladder,
Determination,
And long arms.
The top rung
Would lean on
The shelf of clouds
I could zip up
Grab a star
(With gloves – they're hot!)
And put it high
Near the ceiling
(Don't want the cat to bat at it!)
So I can drift off to sleep
Staring at its tiny perfection
But if I did
It would not go unnoticed
There'd be one less light
High above in the sky
Which would be left
Dimmed, darker, lacking,
Leaving a black hole
Desert dead in its place
Playing tricks with the eye
Like a swirling drain
Growing huge beyond reason
Threating to overtake
Its vicinity (and then some)
Also, it should be said
There'd be one less star
Up there shining brightly

For everyone to enjoy
So I leave them undisturbed
For the greater good
Of all involved
And when I want to sleep
Under the stars
I climb the nearest hill,
Lay back on my pillow,
Appreciate the universe,
And my place within it.

                    February 22, 2013
                    Benson, Vermont

Because if I placed a tiny twinkling real-life star on a low shelf, the cat definitely would go after it.

Our Manifested Destiny

So prominently displayed
So often held up
And looked up to
Yet
So often ignored
And overlooked
By its keepers
The symbol raised and revered
While the real thing rusts and ruins
Fooling nobody
The dream replaced with reality
Faded and tattered
Plundered to its last
Until nothing but
The flavorless husk
Of the former glory remains
Of our manifested destiny
From sea to shining sea, amen

February 22, 2013
Benson, Vermont

Our country is bankrupt (fiscally and politically) from decades of
abuse by those who were put in charge to improve things. No
wonder dystopian novels are so hot because sadly, that's where it
seems we're headed.

Peanut Shell

Quiet, unassuming
Overachieving
Peanut shell
Tough, determined
Unyielding
Until someone managed
To apply enough pressure
And it cracked
Spilling the contents,
Quickly devoured,
Completely used up,
And the empty shell fell,
Hitting the dirty deck
The past successes forgotten
The future plans abandoned
There on the bar floor
As the oft-frequenters casually
Stepped, splintered, crushed
What little remained
Until an underpaid hourly
Swept the remnants away

February 24, 2013
Benson, Vermont

Counting Zeroes

Unbeknownst to me
When I was just a baby
I was dipped and blessed
By a man later accused
Of crimes and removed.
Fast forward forty finds the church
Attempting to number their followers
By including me in their figures…
If I could make a suggestion:
Try to focus on weekly attendance
For those parked in pews –
Stop counting baptized babies
Since you may as well be counting zeroes
Because we're not there anymore.

February 26, 2013
Benson, Vermont

The Catholic Church counts me among their "1.2 billion"
followers despite me having not gone to mass since I was nine. If
they were to count actual weekly attendance, that number would be
a weightless shadow of a fraction of their current estimate.

Note: The "forty" was an exaggeration that worked well with the
words. I'm only 38.

Impact

The impact of most
Affects their surroundings
Like the weightless shadow
Of a fraction of nothing
Passing over a blade of grass
Never to be noticed again.

The impact of some
Is measured like lunar craters
Marring, scarring, changing,
Altering the visible landscape
Clearly noticeable every night
For all of perceptible history.

The impact of the very few
Draws you in like the crushing gravity
Of the densest neutron star
Overcoming the most powerful resistance
Luring in anything with a passing interest
Blasting out energy for galaxies to see.

February 26, 2013
Benson, Vermont

In my notes for my last poem ("Counting Zeros"), I wrote the
phrase, "weightless shadow of a fraction," and it stuck in my mind
enough to inspire me to write this.

Also, I like space stuff.

I Merely Treaded On The Welcome Mat

At my computer, working,
Listening to music when it happened;
Thinking deeply while thanking life,
Thinking intensely, leading to me being
Inwardly focused to the extent
Where I became aware
I was folding in upon myself
Like some kind of multi-dimension origami
Built upon a chilling arasing
And quickly increasing
As my consciousness lifted
And was pushed in and up
Elevated to an impossible height
Within my head but beyond my body
Rising further still until I felt
I had transgressed physics
Past the physical boundary
I've been bound and obliged to –
Until now
When I exchanged that nonsense
For a radiatingly thankful joyful continuation
Of the presently transcendent future me
Where I merely treaded on the welcome mat
Belonging to the Source of everything

February 26, 2013
Benson, Vermont

Not only did this happen earlier today, but it happened again while writing this. To say it was some sort of "out of body experience" doesn't even begin to describe it; I still felt like I was in me, but so far up and beyond the limits of experience…while at the same time I knew it was barely the distance of a single ant step journeying to the Sun. Oddly, I'm completely at ease with this and see no need to question or be concerned by it. It is what it is. Thinking back on it, I will say what now remains is a deep peace with everything.

Note: arasing is another name for piloerection, which is commonly referred to as "goose bumps."

The Dice Have No Memory

Play the game, roll it,
Now, again, and more
Rolling, repeating
Hoping to hit it big
But the numbers
Aren't turning up
Not quite right
So close, but
You don't worry
Because in your mind
Your luck is building up,
For every bad throw
Two good rolls are coming
Like some kind of cosmic bank
With a vested stake in your game
Ready to pay 200% interest –
But chance doesn't work that way
And contrary to what you may think
The dice have no memory

February 27, 2013
Benson, Vermont

I saw the title phrase somewhere and was inspired to write because a surprising number of people don't seem to understand how chance works.

Yawning Off The Winter

A light step would crack and break
The crusty-sharp brittled uneven edge,
Faint remnants of the waist high snow
Melting, receding from the sidewalk
Leaving behind
Pooling puddled water
Dribbling and drabbing
Here and there among the low spots with the
Muddy ground yawning off the winter with squishy elasticity
Soggy tan noodles of grass discolored by the buried months
Looking lifeless under the shallow surface
Of this temporary time between the seasons
Where inspiration is so difficult to find

> February 28, 2013
> North Adams, Massachusetts

Kari was in a meeting with her publisher so I walked across the street from Mass MoCA to the tiny park where the suspended, cut-in-half, boulder is. I took a few pictures, sat on a bench, and took notice of the melting ice, the puddles, and what was underneath.

MARCH

Bridge Preservation

Some wield torches
Swinging them about
Needlessly, scarily, and carelessly
Singeing, blackening, and blistering –
Doing damage and not caring
To everything they happen upon,
Practicing a small-minded policy
Of emotional scorched earth
While being oblivious to
The future implications
This attitude holds

Others, however, have
An open and wide mindset
And are more focused
On bridge preservation
Because you're aware
That this world is small
And you never know
When you're going to need
To double-back a bit
Into familiar territory
To get where you're going,
Or to avoid a damaging flood;
Both of which
Are complete impossibilities
For the limiting careless
Who might get ahead for a while
But there will come a time
When there are no more bridges
Because they've burned them all
And will be stuck in a confining cell
Made from the rigid
Steel-like bars of regret
With walls framed and built
By their choices
Preventing them from advancing

But still allowing them to see
And dwell in distress

> March 2, 2013
> Benson, Vermont

I read the words "bridge preservation" in Danielle LaPorte's book, *The Fire Starter Sessions* and was inspired.

The Lullish Quagmire Of Doubt

"I don't know where to start
I don't know what I know
I don't know what to do."
So here I stand swaying
Nervously, fitfully, despairingly,
And completely unready
Due to my poisonous mindset
Keeping me stuck and mired
In the lullish quagmire of doubt.

Act.
Do something –
Anything!
Most importantly:
Do it right now.
Rise up from the comfortable and warming swaddle of not
knowing
Strike down the constant pressure of not doing
Overcome the inaction
Become what you most want
Don't listen to the decades of sabotaging self-doubt
You can reach it, have it, achieve it – anything you desire
Climb out of your comfort
Expand and grow
Into and beyond
The dreams you dared
Of your greatest self.

March 3, 2013
Benson, Vermont

I just finished *The Fire Starter Sessions* by Danielle LaPorte. It's a very inspiring book, and as I was reading the last few chapters, I set the book aside (very difficult) and wrote a few poems based on, and adapted from, lines I read in the book.

Balancing Is An Act

They say, "To find happiness
You need to achieve balance
To keep life in equal measure,"
But...
"Balancing" is an act,
A myth made quotable
By those who resist change,
Often inadvertently
Performing verbal sabotage
By slowing, abating, decreasing
The competition through
Their trite and tired expressions.
Wake up,
Shake off the sayings,
Light a fire under your feet,
And get going
As fast as you can.
Your dreams are out there
And you need to move to reach them.
You can't get ahead
When you spend your focus
Standing in one spot
Seeking balance
Because in the end,
You will find nothing
But regret.

March 12, 2013
Benson, Vermont

I was inspired by Danielle LaPorte's book, *The Fire Starter Sessions* and what she had to say about balance.

Ninja Rail

Dinner in a busy small-town diner
The waitress was taking an order
From a nearby table asking,
"…and to drink?"
To which, the guy replied, "Ninja rail."

My mind spun thinking, and it took me a moment
To realize the ambient diner background sound
Garbled the request between his lips and my ears
And made a simple ginger ale
Sound so much more fascinating.

March 13, 2013
Castleton, Vermont

Overheard at the Birdseye Diner.

One-Way Fight

We're entrenched in a battle
A terrible knock-down, drag-out
The kind where no one wins
Probably, sadly, because
I'm the only one who knows
About our one-way fight

> March 19, 2013
> Benson, Vermont

I just overheard Kari talking to a friend on Skype and joked that she's having a one-way fight with someone who has no idea.

The Waterfalling Cliff

Pretenses dropped,
The essential us revealed
Exploring the new landscapes
Under the cover of electrical storms
Commissioning our primary motivation
Of becoming vigorously active amid
The continuing echoing joyous rapture
Longingly up, building skyward,
Curving rapidly over the edge
Of the waterfalling cliff
Landing breathlessly into
The tranquil pool of placidity
Drifting off, down, and away

March 19, 2013
Benson, Vermont

Penny On The Tracks

Thoughts steaming along
Powering the piston-like fingers
Pounding along the keyboard
Laying down sentences
Blurring along the lines
Building paragraphs of complexity,
Meaning, depth, and substance

A voice offering contemplation
Talking to me from the periphery
Like a penny on the tracks
Interrupting the drive
Disrupting the momentum
Dividing my thoughts like an axe
Skidding the progress off the tracks
Flying off focus in another direction
Derailing the inspiration
Crashing my concentration
Increasing the frustration
Wrecking my motivation
Stranding me in this nowhere place
Standing in my literary shambles
Cursing the ease at which this happens
Wondering what it will take
To clean up, get back on track,
And get going again

> March 26, 2013
> Benson, Vermont

All it takes is for someone to start talking while I'm writing to
completely derail me.

The Brighter Section Of Carpet

The brighter section of carpet
Right beside the faded part,
Lighter hue, shabby down, and trod upon;
The newer-looking is
So close but so free,
Having managed to escape
The well-worn fate
Due to its out-of-the-way
Location, location, location

March 28, 2013
Rutland, Vermont

Just thinking out loud here but maybe that's why some people look so much younger than their peers, or actual years.

Waiting Room Talker

Waiting room talker actively engaging
Listening in on everyone's conversations
Injecting his favorite tired expressions
Offering his unasked-for thoughts
Being friendly and nice with a dab of annoyance –
Trying to avoid his radar lock-on gaze
Pretending to be busy with my phone
Checking my email for the fifth time
Waiting and ready to exit his presence
Hoping for the nurse to come along,
Calling my name, and saving me

March 28, 2013
Rutland, Vermont

Early Spring Weekday Morning

Early spring weekday morning
Driving past mile-wide fields
Seasonally between white and green
Instead holding fast to the dead color of khaki
And I imagine a thousand surly service workers
Looking leg-less from the waist down
Blending in and not caring
Just watching me drive by,
Texting their friends,
And glaring

March 28, 2013
Benson, Vermont

Kind of an odd visual, but I saw this big field and couldn't help but
to think that thought.

Double Hug

In the lowest, coldest part
Of all that you are
Lies two friends working together
Dual portions of the singular job
Springing your step
Keeping you warm
The socks double hug your ankles
And say, "I got you!"

March 28, 2013
Benson, Vermont

For some reason, I think this is the kind of thing Emily Dickinson would have written if the teenage her wrote poems and lived in 2013.

Or…maybe not.

Water Makes Its Stand

On the surface things are smooth,
Placid, perfect, and beautiful
When closely scrutinized with a microscope
Fissures and cracks become visible
There's where the water collects
Deep inside, laying low,
Helping to fill the unseen spaces, unnoticed
When the temperature dips
When the colder months come
When the frigid standoffishness of winter arrives
Is when the water makes its stand
When it asserts its essentiality to life
And changes from fluid and easygoing
To unrecognizably hard and unyielding
It expands, causing cracks and upheaval
Forever breaking the formally flawless features
Into a bumpy, scarred, and crumbly mess

                    March 28, 2013
                    Benson, Vermont

The Immeasurable Present

We live in the immeasurable present
A time
So not-there narrow,
So quarter-thought thin,
And so mostly-completely nonexistent
Compared with the past and the future
Which extend off in impossible directions of immensity
Like riding the wave
Of fanning the pages
Of a hundred trillion-volume encyclopedia
With no time to digest the passages
And if you think too deeply
About what you're doing
You risk slipping between
Never to be seen again

March 28, 2013
Benson, Vermont

Time can be measured in billionth of seconds, but the thing is we don't think that fast. So I need to ask, at what place does our conscious lie? At some odd place made up of the very tail-end of the future, the razor-thin present, and the just-happened past? I don't know, but I would like to understand this better.

APRIL

Fool Me

Fool me once:
Shame on you
Fool me twice:
Shame on me
Fool me today:
It's expected
And totally ok

April 1, 2013
Benson, Vermont

A Quiet Onlooker

I'm an observationalist
Witnessing human nature
And nature's naturalness
I'm not a conversationalist
Choosing to be a quiet onlooker
With an eye for the unseen
While declining to be an engager
I take only thoughts
And leave nothing behind
To say I was there
Other than bits of words
Written in loose verse

April 1, 2013
Benson, Vermont

I look, observe, notice, and record. I saw a nifty quote on a Tumblr
I follow: "You own everything that happened to you. Tell your
stories. If people wanted you to write warmly about them, they
should've behaved better." I wish I knew who to attribute it to, but
it is so spot-on.

Stressful Pressure

Workers
On edge
Extra fast
Oddly apologetic
Flitting nervously
Eyeing suspiciously
The woman
Wearing the metal name badge
Pinned to a too-crisply white shirt
With an embroidered logo
The woman
Who waited on me
In a too-perfect scripted cadence
Who offered suggestions
Of new items on the menu
Who attempted to upsell
Old items not selling well
The woman
Who was not aware
Her presence disrupted
The normal swing of things,
Her perfection created
A stressful pressure
For the employees,
And for the customers
Standing in line behind me

April 2, 2013
Fair Haven, Vermont

I'm only guessing the woman was something like a regional
manager, but when I walked into this McDonald's a few minutes
ago I became acutely aware of a feeling of everyone being on
edge. The darting eyes of the unusually fast-moving employees
kept landing on this one woman, who I quickly figured out was the
source of the stress.

Crescent Sideswipe

Crescent sideswipe
Slippery smooth angle
Catching the moonlight
Grabbing my attention
Attracting my hand
Despite being deadlier
Than a scimitar's curve
I can't stop handling,
Feeling along the fast arc
Drawing me in
Like an enticing smile

April 3, 2013
Benson, Vermont

I wrote this last night in my sleep. At 2am, I half woke up with the phrase "crescent sideswipe" forefront in my mind, and I barely managed to type it into my phone's notepad. I was falling asleep when the next line floated up and I struggled to type that as well. This continued until the poem was written.

Moved Past The Past

Wrapped tightly in a prison of
Her own choices
Proudly wearing the drama of
Craved attention

Cast off with a shrug of
Indifference
Let loose with no further
Expectations
Moved past the past with
Liberation
Breathed happy with a sigh of
Exhilaration

April 4, 2013
Benson, Vermont

There are times when a part of your past gets all frothy, demanding attention, clinging desperately to the way things were while lamenting the onward pressing of time. That's when it feels really good to just shrug it off, put the past behind you, and press on to the future of your own choosing.

The High Road

Sometimes you need
To take the high road
Which is more expensive
But has a better view
And gets you there
With a deeply noticeable
Emotional calmness

April 5, 2013
Benson, Vermont

Um, why wouldn't you want to take the high road? It seems like the all-around better place to be.

The Wildlife Below

Bright sunlit clouds
Swirling above the striking face
Of the mountain
Eyes trace down the peaks
Playfully obscured in the shadows
To the wildlife below

April 5, 2013
Benson, Vermont

Blended And Rose

A week ago, the land around
Was bleached a deadened gold
Several days of sun and warmth
Saw the life-green color returned
As it blended and rose through
The ground and tinted my thoughts
Of the season changing around me

April 5, 2013
Benson, Vermont

One of Kari's friends in Portland, Oregon posted a picture of a
blooming flower-covered tree on her Instagram and wrote, "Spring
changes everything." That was a few weeks ago, and here in
Vermont, I'm just seeing evidence of that today.

Keep Tuning In

News as entertainment
Fear, anger, terror, horror,
Boxed, presented, and quoted
With baseless speculation
In an unprofessional
And biased manner
From plastic-looking people
Hired for their looks
Rather than their experience
Hoping you'll buy into it,
Feed on the fear,
And keep tuning in –
Maintaining the ratings and
Ensuring nothing changes

April 6, 2013
Benson, Vermont

Popcorn Ceilings

Popcorn ceilings
Are not tasteful at all
In either the culinary
Or stylistic sense

April 6, 2013
Benson, Vermont

I should know. I'm sitting under one right now.

Bigoted Old Man

Bigoted old man
Hanging out at the
Chain fast food place
Like it's his living room
Nursing a large Coke
And the anger in his heart
Clinging to outdated thoughts
Not seen in normal society
In the past sixty years
Commenting on topics such as:
"Those broads,"
"The queers,"
And "shit-ass countries."

The world will be
A much a better
And happier place
When this way of thinking
Dies out through attrition.

April 6, 2013
Benson, Vermont

The old guy I saw at McDonald's the other day was mostly normal, just talking with his friend…except every few minutes his words were punctuated with terrible comments about one group of people or another.

The Lowers

We all know the low people
The negatives who dress themselves
With anger and contrived outrage
Seeing everything through glasses
Tinted with perpetual fear,
Coming from a place where
Lacking and jealousy is a sport,
Immaturity is a way of life,
And harsh words are all they speak.
The lowers who seemingly make up
The old majority of our country
And who aren't lessening their grip
Until it's pried from their cold dead hands.

April 7, 2013
Benson, Vermont

A continuation of that last poem combined with thinking about people who choose to mire their lives with negativity, and how it only begets more negativity.

Make It A Point

Wake up
And make it a point
To see, sense, and feel
To notice the details
Overlooked in the everyday living
To feel the cold fork
To smell the breakfast
To hear the cars passing by outside
To be more perceptive
To your surroundings
To take in everything
And be thankful for it

April 7, 2013
Benson, Vermont

When you make a conscious decision to be perceptive to the world around you, life feels so much richer.

Wet Shoulder Sneeze

Suddenly involuntarily
Deep breath intake
Gearing up for a doozy
No stopping the motion
Can only watch it happen
Limit reached, locked,
Trigger fingered – fired
Wet shoulder sneeze
Splattered something
Yuck, gross, awful
In a spectacular
And echoing way

April 8, 2013
Benson, Vermont

Yuck.

The Western Pull

I identify with where I am
This region of New England
Berkshires-born, Boston-lived,
Spent years in New Hampshire,
My current address in Vermont,
Overnights in Connecticut, the Cape,
And much love for time in Maine
But despite my upbringing and past
I cannot deny the duality of feelings:
The been-there, done-that boredom
That comes with over-familiarity
And the strongly magnetic power
Of the Western Pull, calling, drawing,
Enticing, me to the Pacific Northwest
As it has been for a decade and a half
Slowly building until I am forced
To concede defeat, give in and
Be far-flung across a continent
To a brand new life awaiting me
Full of friends, adventures, and joy
Previously unknown in old New England

April 8, 2013
Benson, Vermont

Things are lining up.

Some Things Shouldn't Be Ignored

Some things shouldn't be ignored
Like the inner voice in your heart
Saying what you know to be true
Telling you what you most want
Showing you the way to happiness
To deny that voice
Is to deny the essential you

April 8, 2013
Benson, Vermont

Cutting The Connection

For maximum productivity
I've found the golden key:
Cutting the connection
To the Internet for a bit
Ignoring the endless links
And the ceaseless clicks
Instead focusing some time
On the matters of your mind
Enriching your introspection

April 8, 2013
Benson, Vermont

I wanted to try something a little different and rhymey.

Happy-Go-Lucky Miracle Dog

Happy-go-lucky miracle dog
Comes equipped with an inner warmth
Which can melt glaciers with a cuteness
That can stop and "aww" the most hardened of hearts
With a ceaseless thwapping tail
Built like a perpetual motion machine
Fitted inside a little tube-like body
That can heft nature's biggest heart
With a determination that easily
Vaults over the tallest obstacle powered by
A love wider than anyone has ever known

April 9, 2013
Benson, Vermont

Written about our miniature dachshund, Charlie Parker. A couple
of years ago, he had a back issue that paralyzed his back legs. We
got him a cart, and within a few weeks, he had miraculously healed
completely to where he was running on all four legs with
boundless energy everywhere. A month ago, he got a standard
rabies shot through a rabies clinic put on by the town, and he had a
severe reaction. Judging from the symptoms he was having, it
seemed certain he would be dead by morning. I spent most of the
night checking on him. After the sun had risen, I was woken up by
him pouncing on my chest and licking my face with his
perpetually-wagging tail. This little guy is so happy all of the time,
it's no wonder he always pulls through.

Managing Coincidences

Coincidences are coming at a questionable rate
Too quickly, too frequently to really be called such
But in actuality I don't know what else to call them
So I spend my time managing my coincidences
Keeping them sorted and organized
By time, subject, and sheer power
Because what else can I really do?
Ignoring them is an impossibility
So I acknowledge their existence,
Thank the universe for the reminder,
File the recurrent event away,
And continue along my coincidental path

April 9, 2013
Benson, Vermont

Horsing Around

All of this horsing around
Has given me pause
And a false sense of beef

April 9, 2013
Benson, Vermont

Inspired by the "what you thought was beef was actually horsemeat" scandal in Europe from last month.

Slips In For A Night

During this transitional month,
If you're awake and observant,
You can bear witness to the event
When the snow slips in for a night
Fast on the back of the fleeting cold
And be treated, for an hour or so,
To falling flakes reminding you
Of the season freshly in your past
Pushed out by the growing greenery
And not to be seen again until the fall

April 10, 2013
Benson, Vermont

Unpacking The Groceries

When unpacking the groceries
And putting everything away
Pick up the bag of dog treats
With *Operation*-like finesse
For even the faintest crinkle
Of the slick-firm plastic
Brays like an alarm
Betraying your movement
To every dog in the house
Alerting them to the
Impending issuance
Of their favorite treats

> April 10, 2013
> Benson, Vermont

Move quietly and carefully. All it takes is one crinkle and you're instantly surrounded by dogs demanding treats.

The Measure Of Success

Despite what we're often told
There is no standard gauge
Telling us where we stand
On the measure of success
There's no way to tell
If we're successful or not
Compared to someone else
Since it's such a relative term.
Success to one
Might be sealing a million-dollar deal
Someone else would say
It's getting through the week without quitting their job.
Success to another might be
Walking past the liquor store without buying.
And some still, have no measure at all
Instead choosing to reject the trappings of such lofty goals.
The summation of these
Tell us to put away our rulers
And not contrast and compare
The things that don't really matter
In the grand scheme of things.

April 11, 2013
Benson, Vermont

The Hardwired Reaction

The origin of humanity
Can be found in a smile
The hardwired reaction
To the positive good
The joyful foundation
To all things we know

April 11, 2013
Benson, Vermont

(=

Lit Marbles

Looking out the window
Down towards the road
Watching the rain
As it steadily fell
Reflected light
Blinked for attention
And caught my eye

Big drops of water
Hung like lit marbles
Swaying slightly
Under the power line
Capturing my thoughts
Making me wonder
If they always did this
And I just never noticed

April 11, 2013
Benson, Vermont

Just In The Shadow Places

The miniature mountains
Long, tall, and irregular
Towering over yawning ants
Are a rare find these days
Just in the shadow places
Hiding, protecting them from
The direct rays of death
Beaming from the distant bulb
But each day forward
Dissipates them further
Until the squishy-ground day
When nothing remains
But the level land it sat upon

April 11, 2013
Benson, Vermont

The large snow bank by the side of the house finally melted the other day.

Opalistic

Flecking colors
Shimmery shining
Capturing attention
Brilliantly entrancing
Making me ogle the
Opalistic oval

April 12, 2013
Benson, Vermont

I'm reading a book by Wayne Dyer and the margins have strips of color, some of which look like opals. When I saw it, I thought it looked "opalistic," which it turns out the spell check does not like one bit.

Only Slightly Dated

Visiting some old music
That I never paid much
Attention to previously
The kind of stuff I used
To dismiss just as filler
And now I'm enjoying it
Like a new-found source
Of spark and inspiration
Only slightly dated in an
Overly nostalgic fashion
Which is something I'm
Not too concerned about
As the pure enjoyment is
Counter-balancing it all

April 12, 2013
Benson, Vermont

I started writing and noticed my lines were all the same length, so I tried to keep that up. It's actually surprisingly limiting (like Twitter) but made me think hard for ways to rephrase lines so they would fit.

Used Silverware For Sale

I'm always surprised when I see
Used silverware for sale
Don't they know that meals
Linger on as memories
Imprinted deeply on our psyche?
Aren't they aware that cutlery's place
As the mid-point,
As the delivery vehicle
In the culinary journey
Is central to the experience?
Before it comes into play
The diner is faced with the meal palate
A mouth-watering mix
Delighting the senses
With stomach-rumbling aromas
Appetizing mix of textures and colors
Radiating the ideal hot and cold
Salivating in anticipation
At the sound of the silver
Clinking, tingling, clanging
As those assembled
Lift the implements,
Feel their familiar
Smooth and raised surfaces
Fit comfortably and expectantly
In their actioning hands
As they apply their purpose
To resize, collect, and lift
The visual feast before them
Losing the view as it passes
From a sight to behold
To a taste in the midst
Of experiencing,
From potential to kinetic
Deliciousness
As the tastes and flavors,
Textures and temperatures

Are sampled, savored,
Processed, and passed on
While the hands act again
With the aid of the implements,
The ones used by a family
Day and day again
For generations
Until today
When their perceived monetary value
Outweighed the years of faithful service
And the millions of memories attached;
The kind of thing that rightfully
Doesn't belong in anyone else's hands
But the ones whose generational retentions
Are firmly imprinted in each knife, fork, and spoon.

April 12, 2013
Benson, Vermont

One of the saddest things is seeing silverware for sale.

From March To April

The transition from March to April
Can send the temperature bouncing
Like the dot on an EKG machine
From hot to cold and back again
Like the whims of a crazy person
Uncertain of which way to go;
Clothes-sheddingly warm one day,
Scraping your windshield the next
And sadly, lately, Mother Nature
Has not only gone off her meds
But is on a bender for the ages
Leaving us to clean up the mess
That we started by being the ones
Responsible for her condition

April 13, 2013
Benson, Vermont

I started out intending this to go in a different direction, but I like
where it went much better. Neat.

Poetry By The Rules

I was looking up poetry groups
In a far-off city I hope to visit
And came across something
That made me scratch my head
And wonder what's going on in theirs.

I was faced with
A list of rules,
Can and can't do's,
Of what types of poetry
Their members
Are not allowed to write,
In addition to submitting
Yourself and your work
And being judged worthy
To gain hallowed entry
Into their select group.

Elitism in poetry
Dictating how it must be done
Goes against the fluid nature
And free-form expression
Of this ancient art form
And not something to be
Constrained and contained
By those who demand you do
Poetry by the rules –
Their rules.

Thank you, but no.
I'll forge ahead
On my own,
Alone and happy
With my way
Of doing things
The way I see fit.

April 13, 2013
Benson, Vermont

Sure, any group can set whatever criteria they want for their members, but come on! It's like a group for graphic designers saying that in order to join you can never have made anything using the color orange.

An Alarm Test For Dogs

Snow falling off the roof
Is like an alarm test for dogs
One sliding section of slush
Sets them off like an intruder,
Or the anticipated arrival
Of an overdue owner

April 14, 2013
Benson, Vermont

Grateful

Grateful for the joy
Thankful for the love
Appreciative for everything
Given from above

> April 14, 2013
> Benson, Vermont

I'm trying to make a conscious effort to be for thankful and express gratitude.

Sleepy Chin

The weight of the hours press and dull
The barely present, slightly open eyes
Sleepy chin in the heel of the hand
Bearing more weight as the head
Clouds up and drifts off...
Until a noise startles and awakens
Resetting the repeating process

April 14, 2013
Benson, Vermont

This is me right now, and sadly it's only 9:30 a.m.

Tickets For Tonight

Tickets for tonight
Pinned to my lamp
A concert, for once
The unripped potential
Those pieces of paper hold
Swirl in my head
Making me dizzy
With anticipation
To see musicians
Whose music inspires me,
And my writing, every day
To feel the bass thumping
Through my whole body
To hear feedback screaming
Ringing loudly in my ears
To have the drums pounding
Moving my head in time
To traffic with the crowd
Like a living thing crowded around
To be singing along with songs
That move me in my daily routine
As they are performed right there
In front of me, for me, live

April 14, 2013
Benson, Vermont

Going to see The Joy Formidable tonight. Their songs, especially "Whirring," have been a great motivator for me while writing my Emily Dickinson, Superhero stories. The last time I went to a concert was in August when I saw Of Monsters And Men. It's been far too long.

Devious Hospitality

Eighty years ago
A plan was hatched
Fantastically creating,
Birthing, and releasing
A monster, a legend
Upon the world
Under the secret guise
Of devious hospitality
To bring tourists
To a boring place
They'd never visit
Without the tall tale
Luring them in

April 15, 2013
Benson, Vermont

I read an interesting report from the BBC where people are looking into every claim of the Loch Ness Monster. The first report was a woman who was a local hotel manager, and she ended up reporting the monster many times, and the BBC said it looks like a conspiracy to draw tourists to the area. Sneaky. I don't know why I didn't think of that when I was a hotel manager.

Formidable Joy

Sonically distorted
Rhythmic wall
Blasting the bodies
Of those assembled
With what they want:
Formidable joy

April 15, 2013
Benson, Vermont

We saw The Joy Formidable perform last night. Great show!

Honked At For Doing The Right Thing

At an intersection and observed
The traffic rules to the letter of the law
Honked at for doing the right thing
Trying hard not to look at them
When they pass by or when they get ahead
Don't want to see any negativity
In the form of gestures or yelling
So I ignore them and keep going
While pushing their beep out of my mind

April 16, 2013
Benson, Vermont

I came to a four-way intersection and stopped. I wanted to turn left.
There was a dump truck at the road to my right wanting to turn to
their left. Because they were there first, I came to a full stop and let
them go. The car behind me did not like this and honked at me
because the dump truck was slow in moving. In the past I'd always
instinctively look at the honker and give them a "What gives?"
look, and normally I'd get to see them give me a rage face or flip
me off. Now though, I don't need that. I just completely ignore
people like that. Who needs the negativity? Not me.

When Inspiration Eludes Me

It is very rare
To find a day
When inspiration eludes me
Usually, I find it ready
And waiting when I wake up
But the other times,
The mornings when
It's just not around,
I don't worry –
I know it's out there somewhere
Wanting me to set off in search –
Sometimes it leaves tracks
Which are easy to follow,
Sometimes it's more subtle
Making me inspect everything
Either way, I find it without much fuss
Usually in the form
Of something new or surprising,
Enriching my life amid the chase

April 17, 2013
Benson, Vermont

Sometimes my poems are tapped out of my fingers into the keyboard as is with no editing and they are perfect. This one, ironically enough, required a lot of editing and retyping. I probably could have written three different versions of this same poem by the time I was done.

To Typo Is Human

Awkward mistypes
Here and there
Salted lightly
Throughout my writings
Annoying the perfectoonist
And showing others
To typo is human

April 17, 2013
Benson, Vermont

Do I ever intend to have the occasional typo in my writings? Land o'lakes, no! But, it does happen from time to time, despite my repeated editing. It's the lite curse of being a writer.

I had originally typed, "self-published writer" but I've found typos in professionally published books all the time. It just comes with the territory; if you write a few hundred thousand words, there's bound to be some typos. No biggie.

(And yes, I intentionally spelled perfectionist wrong.)

Hasty Geese

A honking above raises my head
As a close pair of hasty geese
Sleek through the residual sky
Like winged, billed bowling pins

April 18, 2013
Benson, Vermont

I was out for a walk when I saw a pair of geese fly by and I
thought, "Hey, they look a lot like bowling pins."

Time Dresses The Hours

A richly-lived existence is one
In which time dresses the hours
In such a subtle, complex finery
Exquisitely layered and detailed
That, in order to appreciate it fully
To the extent it truly deserves,
One must commit to the cause

April 18, 2013
Benson, Vermont

While on a walk tonight, the first two lines popped into my head from out of nowhere. As I was typing it into my phone, the geese from the last poem flew by.

The Center Of Thought

The center of thought pours forth
From the Source of ideas
From the unknown unseen place
Where everything originates
And where everything returns

April 19, 2013
Benson, Vermont

I am mired deeply in thought on where our thoughts originate.

To Fill The Air

Speculation run rampant
By those making their living
Sitting in front of the cameras
Trying to pass the time
Filling the void
Leading the interviewees
Clarifying and offering
Nothing new or noteworthy
But they prattle on
Struggling to fill the air
With assumptive rehashing
Instead of what once was news

April 19, 2013
Benson, Vermont

Does The Document Hold

How much worth
Does the document hold
When billions are spent
Suppressing
Its basic tenants?

How much power
Does the document wield
When the boots of
Enforcement
Stomp it down daily?

How much respect
Does the document garner
When the citizens
Cherry-pick
Their favorite parts to follow?

How much longer
Does the document have
When major sections are
Invalidated
At the drop of a helmet?

April 20, 2013
Benson, Vermont

Random thoughts on the Constitution. Only partially related, but the other day I saw a striking picture. It showed two small girls sitting on the floor of a library. One was holding a copy of *Little Red Riding Hood* while the other was holding a machine gun. It said, "One child is holding something that's been banned in America to protect them." It went on to say that the book has been banned because of the bottle of wine she carries in her basket in the story. It's frustrating witnessing the continuous counterproductive attempts of the regression of society by specific elements with deep pockets. If they had their way, the movie *Idiocracy* would become a reality.

At The Restaurant For Monsters

On the menu at the restaurant for monsters:
Free-range, grass-fed, gluten-free crafters.
On the menu across the street at the diner:
Fast food-fattened box store greeters.

April 21, 2013
Benson, Vermont

Silly, silly, silly.

Read Those First

There will never be enough time
To read all the books you *want* to read
So instead focus on those
Whose gravity is hard to resist;
The ones that call out to you,
That pull you to them,
That you *must* read.
Read those first.

April 21, 2013
Benson, Vermont

Sometimes I feel overwhelmed when I walk into a bookstore because there are so many books I want to read, but I know I'll never get through them all.

Maybe I need to read faster.

Perpendicular Intelligence

From out of nowhere
Left-angled line
Crashing and cutting
Through into
The mainstream beam
Blasting across
Straight-line thought
Changing everything
Starting from the point
Of intersection onward
The perpendicular intelligence
Left an indelible mark
Waking the masses
Opening the attention
To possible new directions
Tainting the multitudes
With new ways of thinking
Leaving the bulk
Running askew, confused,
And fragmented
Weakening the beam
As lines from within
Turned to one side
Leaving in search
Of something new
To impact with reason

April 22, 2013
Benson, Vermont

I woke up in the middle of the night with the title phrase at the
forefront of my mind.

Sunsetty

Our local heat lamp
Slowly sinking westward
Blinding-bright in warming hues
Casting the ideal rosy glow
Photographers salivate and wait for
On the facing side of things
While the shadowy darkness
Picturesquely painting
Boldly across the landscape
Elongating in relation
To the sunsetty portion
Of the remaining evening

April 23, 2013
Benson, Vermont

Wonder Resurgence

When a one-hit wonder
From two decades ago
Experiences an unexpected
Overnight resurgence
And is at the forefront
Of our normally forgetful
Collective conscience
It is most likely due
To that person dying

> April 23, 2013
> Benson, Vermont

Sad but true.

Aware Of The Present

An aware being
Being aware
Of the present
And the present
I have gotten now
And I now get

> April 23, 2013
> Benson, Vermont

I just read an interview with Eckhart Tolle and something from it clicked in my head, not just with myself, but clicked with a whole bunch of other things I've read and heard – like it was an unifying piece of information that was so hugely simple but at the same time, gigantically profound.

A Bossy Nightlight

Swimming in the shallows of slumber
I turn over to a more comfortable position
And am faced with a narrow bright light
Squinting out the window at the full moon
I close my eyes to block it out, but
It still makes its presence known
Like a bossy nightlight
Starved for attention at 3 a.m.
So I turn my back to it
And try to fall back asleep

April 24, 2013
Benson, Vermont

Hey, moon! Shut up!

Markers Of Lives

When they arrived
When they left
The markers of lives
The dates of existence
Not their works or
Who they were –
That's not what's
Most important;
What is essential
Is that they were here
For a while
Before moving on
And someone,
So long ago,
Wanted them to be
Remembered
For all time

April 24, 2013
Benson, Vermont

My evening walk brings me through a cemetery and last night I spent a while thinking about how headstones just have names and dates and nothing about what they did in life. I know that's probably because they couldn't afford a bigger stone or more words engraved. Still though, I would think if you were going to immortalize someone for all time you would at least put in a descriptive line or two.

Rotated Out Of View

Woke up to the moon
A large and full sight
Minutes later I looked again
Noticing it had slid down
Lower in the window
Which is not really true
Since the moon doesn't move
In the way we normally say;
It rotated out of view
Due to the Earth, who moved

April 25, 2013
Benson, Vermont

646

Everywhere I look
From the shoes on my feet
To the clocks that surround me
And the number of followers
On a new follower's Twitter feed
To the length of "How Soon Is Now"
Over and over, the number I always see
No matter where, no matter what;
License plates, number of comments,
The size of a downloaded file
Several times daily
It's always the same:
646

April 27, 2013
Benson, Vermont

I think everyone has numbers that seem to follow them around.
Back when I started in hotels, the front desk computer system
required a password to sign in. It could be any amount of numbers
or letters. After seeing people trying to type the whole name of
something as their password and realizing how inefficient it was, I
chose "646" because I could type it super quick on the number
pad. For about ten years I used that as my work password (until I
worked with a different computer system that had tougher
password requirements). Ever since, I've seen the number 646
almost on a daily basis to the point where I just take it as a given.
Last year I was buying a new pair of New Balance walking shoes
on Amazon when I saw that the model number was 646 and it was
even sewn into the heel of the shoe. Anyway, I saw the number
this morning and thought I should write something about it.

Revisioning

Things in mind, replaying
Forward front and backwards
Reviewing and reseeding
From every angle
But the more I rewatch
The more new things
Get added into the mix
Aspects that weren't there
Previous to the repeating
Revisioning it into
An idealized view

April 28, 2013
Benson, Vermont

I started with a completely random phrase and went with it to see where it would go. My spell check is also telling me that "revisioning" is not a real word…and with two clicks it's been added to my dictionary.

Wisps Of Smoke

Wisps of smoke
Exhaled like a too-deep thought
Thankfully released
Tendrils lifted and carried
By the light breeze
Expanding, widening
Too quickly to appreciate
Before vanishing like years
At a point too close for comfort

> April 28, 2013
> Benson, Vermont

I left out the bit that this took place in a cemetery this evening
while Kari and I were discussing at which point do we give up on
biology and give in to the thought that we may never have our own
children.

Plump Comma

A ball of something
Floating in the sky
Grabs my attention
And brings it to the
Bird on a phone line
Like a plump comma
Sitting and resting
Surveying things
From up on high

April 29, 2013
Benson, Vermont

This mourning dove really did look like a plump comma for a second.

Will Trade Coffee For Gossip

A small-town diner
With kitschy signs
Showing cartoony scenes
From the 50s
And others with silly phrases.
The two men at the counter
Haven taken one at face value
"Will trade coffee for gossip"
As they delve deep into the affairs
Of anyone and everyone
With any sort of
Connecting commonality
Working hard for the mugs
Of hot coffee in their hands.

April 30, 2013
Ticonderoga, New York

For my birthday today, we took an impromptu trip over to the town of Lake George and found that the area was mostly closed since it seems to be very seasonal. We drove up and around the lake, stopping for lunch in Ticonderoga, New York.

Dachshunds Are The Accordions Of The Pet World

Dachshunds are the accordions of the pet world
Playing their parlance
With due respect
Meanwhile, elsewhere in the universe:
Accordions are the dachshunds of the music world
Signifying the semblance
Of something greater

April 30, 2013
Benson, Vermont

Uh, I don't know what I think about this one. It's kind of out there. I started out with the two main declarative lines, which I liked the imagery of, but I'm not sure about where it ended up. I might re-write this at some point down the road.

A Place That's Easy To Be

A distant city calls to me
So I spring into action
From green New England,
The only home I've known,
Across the drought-lands,
Landing near the Pacific
Where my mind
Settles in among
So many similar
And like-minded souls
Finally able to relax
And be the real me
In a place that's easy to be

> April 30, 2013
> Benson, Vermont

I've never been there, but the pull is too great to ignore.

MAY

Wraps And Clings

The humidity wraps and clings
Like a fumbly drunk ex-lover
Pawing, groping, hanging on
Partly out of desperation
Acting hard to heat things up
Partly due to necessity
Pulling close to fight gravity
Delivering hot breath-slurred whispers
Saying the right things
But in the wrong way
As I lean away dripping hot
From the thickly oppressive pressure
It makes no matter where I go
It's there, wrapping me tight
Making things uncomfortable

May 3, 2013
Benson, Vermont

It hasn't been humid, but it has gotten warm lately. We went from daily temperatures in the 40s and 50s to 70s and 80s practically overnight. The pre-summer warmth made me think of humidity and I thought it might be interesting to personify it.

Buying A Box Of Dimmer Bulbs

Flipped the switch
And was rewarded
With nothing at all.
I replaced the bulb
With one borrowed from
A rarely-used lamp
And was taken aback
By how intensely bright
The bathroom became
Showing every cranny
On the faces in the mirror
Illuminating the things
That previously had been hid
By the weak wattage
Of the old bulb.

The following day,
Upon the wife's orders,
I'm at the hardware store
Buying a box of dimmer bulbs
To replace the replacement
Because it did its job too well.

> May 4, 2013
> Benson, Vermont

True story.

Our Anniversary

Some may think
Cinco de mayo
Is the festivity
But in reality
Everyone is celebrating
Our anniversary

> May 5, 2013
> Benson, Vermont

Happy 6th anniversary!

Thoughts Through The Gray

Bored while working
Makes the mind go turning
Around a few times
In place behind the face
Until gravity takes over
Pulling my attentions closer,
Bending my intentions
Down the steeply inclined slope
Leading to the comforting place
Shrouded in uplifting darkness
The place where the other me
Winks, nods, and takes over
Tossing himself, person, and
Thoughts, through the gray
Resurfacing on the other side
In the redly-lit wondrousness
Of the stirring consciousness
Steeped in the currency
Of nuanced sensory exchange
Where everyone's a billionaire,
The exchange rate is reciprocally beneficial,
And trading is quickly brisk
Among the hardly and fully acquainted
Which is a matter of no importance
As long as the mutual mindset is in place
Resulting in a brightly scenic wonderful world
That beats the pants off the drab workplace
I had previously found myself confined within

May 6, 2013
Benson, Vermont

Your work environment can make a world of difference.

The Day Became Long With Anger

Despite the cheery outside
Feelings were falling inside
As escalating words
Rose and sped in matched tones
Before the mutually storming retreat
Allowing the pressure cookers
Time to replay the boiling events
Simmering in their separate rooms
And the day became long with anger

May 6, 2013
Benson, Vermont

A few days ago Kari said something along the lines of the title line, so I wrote it down and did something with it.

Whim Of The Wind

The sky spaces
Bluing through and between
The tree's leaves
Forming faces
Furrowed brows
Smiling mouths
Swaying slightly
Changing form from
Ominous to cuddly
Happy to snarly
On the whim
Of the ever-changing wind

       May 11, 2013
       Benson, Vermont

Shedding The Shell

Something quite appealing
With moving; leaving
Completely changing coasts
Exchanging history and snow
And this life that has been mine
For damp-dark towering forests
And the me that I will become
Shedding the shell
I've worn for too long
Ditching the things
I'm done dragging around
And walking freely
In the direction I choose

> May 12, 2013
> Benson, Vermont

The Common Bouquet

Often dismissed as weeds
Dandelions,
The common bouquet,
Are always busy
Spending their time spreading,
Splashing a cheery sun-like vibrancy
Across the yards and fields
Throughout the states and counties
Numbering in the billions,
Their yellow-topped blur
Coating and embellishing
The grassy sea of green
Like a bright lemony frosting
Decorating the landscape

May 12, 2013
Benson, Vermont

I love how huge fields are transformed by the blanket-like yellow
covering created by a sea of dandelions.

Like A Tipsy Simile

Like a tipsy simile
Smiling and clicking
Crazily on Facebook
Liking everything
That it likes and sees
Much in the manner
Of a metaphoric something

May 14, 2013
Benson, Vermont

While out for my nightly walk, the first part of this popped into my mind. It's weird and seemingly unfinished, but it is what it is.

I Willed It Real

Today's the day they say
That Emily Dickinson died
I've been to the museum
I've paid my respects
At her fenced-in grave
I'm also aware of the
Hundred twenty seven years
That have passed
Since her passing
But unlike the world
That thinks her dead
I know for a fact
That she's alive
Just as you or I.
How can this be?
Simply, I willed it real
But with a super slant
And a sword on her back
Which was unconventional
Yet also quite necessary
To give her an edge
And a fighting chance
Against a world
Increased and amplified
From what she once knew.
It's a joy to see her thrive
In the slightly modified
Way I've imagined her
And just as long as
People keep reading
She will live forever
Exploring the world
Off on new adventures.

> May 15, 2013
> Benson, Vermont

Emily Dickinson, Superhero is pretty awesome and not bound by silly notions like "death."

Bed Checker

Every hotel
Every time
She has me be
A bed checker
To make sure
It's clean and free
Of all things nasty

May 20, 2013
Boston, Massachusetts

Kari asked me to write about how every time we stay in a hotel she
has me check for bedbugs and errant hairs in the beds, so I did.

I Can Smell The Path The Old Man Took

My crinkled nose knows
Which way he came and
Which way he went
For I can smell the path
The old man took
The layered lane he walked
Was dressed with a stale stench
Practiced, perfected, and put in place
By decades of habit
Filtered through the deadened senses
Puffed, clouded, and shrouded
Trailing behind like a bridal train
Tripping up those unfortunate enough
To cross his wafting contrail

May 20, 2013
Boston, Massachusetts

When someone has been smoking for decades, the smell not only permeates their skin, but it expands and acts like an odiferous footprint.

Duality

A tentative helloing in their native tongue
Hovering over the flowchart in their brain
Waiting for the response
And responding fluently,
In-kind, in the same language
Pauseless and perfect in pitch and tone;
A duality incomprehensible where I'm from

> May 25, 2013
> Montreal, Quebec

I LOVE hearing French spoken in normal everyday life. One of the really neat things about Montreal is how you can walk into a store and the people say, *"Bonjour!"* and if you reply with a, "Hello," they'll instantly respond with an accentless, "Hey," or, "What's up."

Blessless In God's House

While visiting and appreciating
One of the foremost
Cathedrals on the continent
A sneeze overtook a visitor
But her automatic reaction,
Her "Thank you," went unused
As the expected rote response
From those around her
Never came
Despite being surrounded
By hundreds of the faithful
And she went blessless in God's house

> May 25, 2013
> Montreal, Quebec

While visiting the Notre Dame Cathedral, my friend Kimberly sneezed. After a second she realized that not a single person said, "Bless you," or the French equivalent. Weird, because that's the one place you'd expect that people would be a little freer with blessing others.

Love Pew

Overly small church bench
Awkwardly placed to one side
One that can only fit two
Due to the nearby placement
Of a larger-than-normal statue.
It looks kind of like a love seat
If so, would it be called a "love pew?"
I'm not sure, but that seems wrong.
What about naming it a "pewette?"
Yikes, that makes me think of
Something like "moist towelette"
And I'm pretty sure that
Would inevitably lead
To impure thoughts
Which is probably why
They never named
This little pew
To begin with.

May 25, 2013
Montreal, Quebec

Puppy

Today, Puppy,
The kindest, gentlest,
Faithful, mutt of a dog
Who loved eating treats,
Going for long walks,
And adding his thoughts
With a loud, "Woo! Woo!"
Breathed his last
And passed away
After having long ago
Ensured with a nudge of his muzzle
And the constant wagging of his tail
That he, and his loving nature,
Would always be remembered
As he got up from pillow bed
And settled down to sleep
In the bottom of our hearts

        May 26, 2013
        Benson, Vermont

Framed With Perspective

Something in the foreground
Coincidentally
Lining up perfectly
With something in the background
The distant object
Framed with perspective
Visible only from my view
Takes my attention
From the task at hand
As I see things
In a whole new way

May 27, 2013
Benson, Vermont

I do this all the time.

Natural Fireworks

Slow motion
Low altitude
Non-exploding
Annual, natural fireworks
Bursting with color
In waves of daffodils
Volleys of tulips and
Sprays of bleeding hearts
Close to the ground
While endless cascades of leaves
Paint the above with green

> May 27, 2013
> Benson, Vermont

I meant to write this a few weeks ago when I was there, in the season. Those flowers have passed and the late spring/early summer show is starting to rev up.

JUNE

New Shower Curtain

A new shower curtain
Fresh and clean
Like painty vinyl
With rectangular creases
That'll hang out with time
Plasticky appealing
Zippy smooth crinkly
When my fingers
Slide across its surface
Stiffly hanging
Awkward and unwieldy
Filling the bathroom
With the new-curtain-scent
I strangely crave
For a short time
Making my shower
Into something
More interesting
Which only happens
Once every other year

June 6, 2013
Benson, Vermont

Early Bird

Just like times,
Signs have no meaning
To the early bird
A species determined
To get what they want
Regardless of the rules.
Hours early and
Overly pushy
While making promises
Saying they won't be a bother
But instead pester the seller
With countless questions
And ridiculous offers
Taking up their time
Delaying their opening.
To these old crows
The unopened and
Unstarted are already
Corpses to be picked over
For the scant few meaty bits
And leave the bones for others
As they fly on to their next victim.

June 15, 2013
Benson, Vermont

People who show up way early to yard sales are incredibly rude
and disrespectful.

To The Rocks

To the flies
A day is a lifetime
To the trees
A year is a sliverous ring
To the rocks
The seasons
Are barely a blink
To us
A red light is forever

June 27, 2013
Benson, Vermont

I wanted to say something about the elements in our bodies that have existed for billions of years, but I didn't know how to word that succinctly enough to adhere to the simple format of this poem…and that's going to bug me all night because it's the job of a writer (especially a poet) to be able to communicate the unsayable.

The Shortest Night

I watched the evaporating light
On the lightiest night
Where the visual buffet
Is chock full
And freely flowing
With the added accompaniment
Of the nearly full moon
Hanging huge and low
Kind of cheating
By catching and reflecting
The sun's radiance
And adding it into the mix
On tonight
The shortest night

June 28, 2013
Benson, Vermont

On the night of Summer Solstice, Kari and I sat in the old cemetery
on the hill across the street, had wine, and watched the sunset.
While it was happening, I wrote this (but didn't get around to
typing it into my computer until now).

As a side note, I think it's crazy that the word "lightiest" isn't a
"real" word. I should make a Poet's Dictionary that has interesting,
common, and fun variations of words.

Oof

Some songs wield incredible power
It doesn't matter if years have gone by
And their existence has been forgotten
But when they play…
It's like an emotional punch in the gut
With memories and feelings flooding
Amid the wide-eyed "oof"
And sharp intake of breath
When you have to try your best
To remain upright and afloat
And not get carried away
Or suffer down and drown
Surrendering to the situation
Of the blasting volley from the past

June 28, 2013
Benson, Vermont

For the past week or two, all I've listened to is *Random Access Memories* by Daft Punk. I've never been interested in Daft Punk, but wow, it's such an amazing album. Tonight, I thought it might be nice to have a break from that and put on my "Poetry" playlist in iTunes. After a few minutes, I realized that I needed to put more songs into that playlist since it only has 42 songs. I switched over to "Southpaw," my playlist of emotional and deeply-held songs. This is an old playlist I made years ago based on a mix-cd I made myself back in 2000. The song "Spacemilk" by The Sheila Divine came on and I felt the emotional wallop that this song has, and started writing. There's nothing emotional actually associated with that song for me, but the lyrics, Aaron Perrino's voice, and the music is a powerful combination.

JULY

Hot Breeze Path

The air, moist and gloppy
My skin, more of the same
Crackers, rendered soft and inedible
Clothes, sloppy and in need of changing
Sweltering in this heat and humidity
Showering becomes useless a moment later
Everything running slower and slicker
Wishing back for the frigid months
Which seem light-years distant
Until they come again, I'll take refuge
Sitting in mild discomforting relief
Found in the hot breeze path of a box fan

> July 3, 2013
> Benson, Vermont

Hot, humid, and a daily thunderstorm is Florida weather, not Vermont weather.

Its Singular Purpose

Oversized pickup truck
Revving loudly to attract attention
Ridiculously huge tires
Burning rubber down the road
Below the flaming custom paint job
Blazing across the chrome-detailed side
Twin exhaust stacking straight up
From the back, belching and brapping
Dark clouds lingering like a bad taste;
The driver, hat on backwards
With his arm out the window,
Holding the side of the truck
As if he's attempting to hug it,
Thankful for its singular purpose:
Giving meaning to his existence

> July 3, 2013
> Fair Haven, Vermont

Sometimes I think that if people really took the time for some inner reflection and deep introspection, they'd discover something inside of them that would shine greatly all by itself without the need for giant garish toys to attract attention. Might as well replace the "pissing Calvin" and area code window stickers (why is this even a thing?) with one that says, "The only way I know of to get attention from others is by driving this monstrosity."

Jubilation, Expressed In Explosive Form

The echoing jubilation,
Expressed in explosive form
Reports across the valley
With a series of
Bangs and booms,
Sizzles and crackles,
In singles and doubles
Until the 20-minute mark
When the God of Celebration
Sits behind His drum kit
And pounds away
As quickly, wildly, and patriotically
As possible, hitting every note
Dozens of times a second
Until the final mortar's thunderous boom
Signals to all about
That the spectacle is over.
Later it is recreated
On a fractional scale
In tipsy backyards
Throughout the night.

                    July 4, 2013
                    Benson, Vermont

Coincidentally, as I finished this, the Peter Gabriel song, "Solsbury Hill" happened to start playing from my playlist and the part, "my heart goin' boom, boom, boom…" went nicely with what I was writing.

Billowy Pillowy Fast

Billowy pillowy fast
Rising through the ceiling
Above the deck
Where clouds stack like mountains
And I feel like an adventurer
Traversing unknown lands

July 10, 2013
On a plane from Chicago to Seattle

Public Fact #1

Public fact #1:
The louder
And more obnoxious
A phone's ringtone is
The slower and longer
It takes for its owner
To hear the noise,
Look around confused,
Recognize the sound,
Locate the pocket,
Withdraw the phone,
Face it right-side up,
Open the case,
Press the button,
And answer the fucking thing

July 12, 2013
Seattle, Washington

A Chance To Absorb

At a Seattle sports bar
That's better known
For really good food
And karaoke at night
There's an old man
Sitting nearby
Staring thoughtfully
At the glass wrapped
In his fingers
Listening in
To the lives and words
As the table of thirty-somethings
Talk unapologetically
About sex, exes, and the Internet
He pretends to watch
The women's soccer match
But his aimed ear betrays him
Just as his mere presence
Is equally telling
Describing a picture
Of a solitary man,
Probably lonely,
Stops in every late afternoon
As a way to connect
A chance to absorb
Youth, life, and human contact
Soaking it all in
Like a dry, brittle sponge
Until, eventually,
After many hours
Of nursing his one beer,
His presence is missing
As he must have
Gotten his fill
And slipped away
Without notice

July 12, 2013
Seattle, Washington

Three of us stopped into a bar to get a drink. The one drink turned into many more, dinner, and karaoke spread out over four hours. For a good amount of that time, an old man sat in the booth beside ours; just sitting there, holding his drink.

Young Love Etched In Wet Cement

Young love etched in wet cement
Two names and a year
Encircled by a heart
Sealing the deal
In the putty-like pliable gray
Given time, this testament of love
Solidified and hardened
As a public declaration
Far outlasting the emotions
That initiated the act
And made this a street
They can no longer walk down

July 13, 2013
Seattle, Washington

After seeing this on a sidewalk, it got me thinking about what
might have happened to the crazy kids who wrote it.

Plussing Three

A lifetime on the East Coast
A week or so on the West Coast
Where every time I saw the time
The addition engine revved up
Instinctively plussing three in my head

> July 13, 2013
> Seattle, Washington

This happened every single time. I wonder how long it'll take for this mental quirk to go away when we move out this way.

Deleted

A walking sad sack.
Overly confident.
Not genuine.
Putting on a show.
Doesn't realize it.
Really hard to be around.
Gets dropped into the spam bin.
Deleted.

July 13, 2013
Seattle, Washington

Actual lines I overheard at a bar of two women discussing a mutual acquaintance they shared. The finality of the last line is the most powerful to me and I've found myself lingering on it. It's almost as if this is their way of electronically killing the person they didn't like.

Corn Tattoo On Her Arm

Corn tattoo on her arm
When asked why
She replied, "I like corn,"
But she's lying
She has to be.
No one gets a life-sized ear
Permanently etched
In such a prominent place
For a food they "like."
I could see if she grew up
On a farm, or came from
A corn-growing region
That would, at least,
Be a proper explanation,
Unlike the one she gave.

> July 13, 2013
> Seattle, Washington

Seriously, I like mashed potatoes (a lot) but I'm not running down
to the local tattoo parlor to get a buttery bowl-full inked into my
bicep.

Friends Before We Met

A coast apart
But close online
This is the way of today
Where we meet people
Through the Internet
And can spend years
Writing to each other
Building a dialogue
Knowing about each other
Cheering their successes
Comforting their falls
And being big fans
Of who they are.
When we finally see them
Face-to-face, in person,
It's like the greeting is a casual
And the hug is a formality
With the people who were
Friends before we met.

> July 16, 2013
> Portland, Oregon

Tonight I met a whole bunch of people that I've been friends with online for a long time (years, in some cases).

Portland Moss

Each telephone pole
On every downtown street
Is covered and coated
By a thick barky layer
Of Portland moss
From four to six feet up
With the faded
And colored,
Unreadable
Bits and chunks
Of events gone by
And long forgotten

July 17, 2013
Portland, Oregon

The Distance Was Nothing

Friends I've only known
Online
I've liked what they've done
On Facebook
I've favorited their words
On Twitter
I've commented on their photos
On Instagram
I've repinned their inspirations
On Pinterest
And, after years of interactions,
We finally met face-to-face...
Which was merely a formality
As we got along like
The distance was nothing

July 17, 2013
Portland, Oregon

During this trip to Seattle and Portland, I've met so many people
I've known online for years and discovered that the distance didn't
matter; we got along amazingly well in person as we did online.

I know this is crazy-similar to the one two poems back, but I'm
keeping this one in because it's showing how various social media
platforms connect us in different ways.

Painfully Easy To Find

If you are looking for me
In the city of Portland
I'm painfully easy to find
Just look for the beardless guy
Who doesn't have any tattoos

July 18, 2013
Portland, Oregon

Theric

Despite being an Eric here
My interest lies elsewhere
Causing me to be theric

July 20, 2013
Benson, Vermont

Dawn's Cracking Smudge

The chiming light of the dawn's cracking smudge
Serves to stir the morning life
Rousing them up into a chirping swirl
Too early to rise and start my day
Too late to get any quality sleep
I lie in bed look out my window
And watch the transitioning colors
Of this morning's waking show

> July 27, 2013
> Benson, Vermont

I found this poem on my phone this morning. I vaguely remember having an idea for a poem and thought that if I didn't write it down, I'd forget it. I don't recall having written it, so I guess I wrote it in my sleep.

Rewired

Certain expectations
Already set high
Were blown away
Reprogrammed to an extent
That she became
Rewired to her core
From that moment on
As the barish standard
Was shot into space
And nothing (nothing)
Was ever the same again

> July 27, 2013
> Benson, Vermont

That word is pronounced "*bar*-ish" not "*bear*-ish." It's not in the dictionary so don't bother reaching for it (unless you're reaching for my special Poet's Dictionary I haven't written yet).

Question Those That Came Before

When you accept
Things as they are
You may as well
Take an axe to the steps
Of human progress
Because the only way
That we, as a society,
Will move ahead
Is to truly question
Those that came before
And dream beyond
Their stagnant present

July 30, 2013
Benson, Vermont

AUGUST

Spiritualize Accordingly

Spirituality is not defined
By a weekly set-time,
Or going through the motions
Of repetitive customs
Handed down over generations
That doesn't coincide
With your own personal views.
Rote memorization and recitation
Is not the same as an active belief structure,
So spend some time reflecting
On what is central to your way of thinking
And spiritualize accordingly.

August 4, 2013
Benson, Vermont

Chillsome

A warm day
Sliding, shifting,
Changing into a cool night
Abounding with
A chillsome freshness
Carefully and fragrantly
Hung in the air
Somewhere below
The blending blue
With darker hues
But above the last firefly
Whose subdued light
Lightly fades into fall

August 7, 2013
Benson, Vermont

Observances at a half past twilight last night.

Heart-Deep In The Quicksand

Seeking serenity
Among the amenities
Where it's easy to think
It will be achieved,
But in the late-night
Awake-hours of
Ceiling-stared honesty
Trapped by the hour
In the painfully aware
Illuminated darkness
Happiness is elusive,
Despite the comfort
And the companion,
Where you are alone
Heart-deep in the quicksand
Of your unsharable thoughts

August 7, 2013
Benson, Vermont

Because I used to be a hotel manager, I'm still interested in, and keep up with, news in the hotel world. I read that the company that I used to work for started a new brand of hotel. That could be why, a few hours later, the first two lines of this poem popped into my mind. I started writing from the point of view of someone who has way too much on their mind. I'm not sure if the "companion" person is their life partner, or just one for the night. Either way, it's adding to the weighty emotional gravity pulling them down. I also like the fact that despite being in a darkened room, that she is lying awake and all of her troubles are fully illuminated. And, hoo-boy, when I was a kid, I was *terrified* of quicksand. It seemed that in the late-70s, early-80s, almost every TV show had the overdone plot device of someone falling into quicksand. I think most everyone has unsharable thoughts, and while writing this poem, I realized those thoughts are probably like suffocating or drowning in quicksand.

Cute-ish

Describing something as
"Cute-ish"
Is also equally implying
That it possesses
Uncute qualities
Which negate its attractiveness

August 7, 2013
Benson, Vermont

A Diminished Commonality

A diminished commonality
Recessed beyond communication
Our only compatibility lies in the past
And I'm not headed in that direction
Anytime soon
Or ever again

August 7, 2013
Benson, Vermont

We have three choices in life: grow, stay stagnant, or regress.

Parlaying The Coppering Reach

Parlaying the coppering reach
Into something hefty
Something lasting
A weighty stability
With a feeling of permanence
Extinguishing any fears
With the heavy blanket
Of comforted reassurance

August 8, 2013
Benson, Vermont

I have no idea what this is about. Sorry.

Dot

Dot
A tiny spot
So small
It's barely seen
Hardly perceptible
Almost unnoticeable
From a distance,
Until you zoom in
And that speck
Grows exponentially
To the size of a planet
Containing all of humanity

August 8, 2013
Benson, Vermont

I was looking at the new "Pale Blue Dot" photo that was taken recently from Saturn, which shows a tiny point of light off in the distance. That dot is Earth.

Humanity's Waist

The future marches steadily toward us
Without pause or rest
But whether or not we become the future
And rise to its full promise
Is dependent on us shaking free
Of the societal regressors
Full-throttle reversers
And dead-weight
Pulling with all their might
On the chain cinched tightly
Around humanity's waist

August 9, 2013
Benson, Vermont

Who knows what we could have accomplished if all of humanity
had worked together instead of doing everything possible to
obtain/cling to a childish notion of "power."

Stars Raining Down

The promised showing
Of stars raining down
Was sadly waylaid
By the thin layer of clouds
Obscuring our hoped view
Where even the brightest
Celestially-placed objects
Were barely visible
Nonexisting any chance
Of being showered
By the reigning Perseids

August 12, 2013
Benson, Vermont

Around nine at night, I walked the dogs and the sky was perfectly clear. Three hours later we went out to see the meteor shower, but saw nothing due to the obscuring layer of clouds that had moved in.

Projection Versus Introspection

On the outside:
Calm, cool, and collected
Like an iconic photograph
Of a James Dean penguin.
On the inside:
Wild erratic and chaotic
Like the flight path of a moth
Atop Mount Washington.

Projection versus introspection
Seeing is believing for others
Feeling is knowing for yourself

August 14, 2013
Benson, Vermont

I love the visual of a James Dean penguin. Also, until recently, the highest wind speed on the planet was recorded on Mount Washington in New Hampshire.

Seeing Your Self-Brilliance

People are intensely more aware
Of their perceived flaws
Than of their most positive traits.
This negative self-image
Keeps the "beauty" industry in business.
Shutter them by seeing your self-brilliance.

August 14, 2013
Benson, Vermont

I can't stress this enough.

Looking Lightly

Life is like walking into a New England general store.
A real one.
The kind that's been in the same location
Since the early 1800s,
With stuff stacked and piled high
In every cranny, shelf, and nook –
With so much that it was impossible to take it all in,
And if you tried, really and honestly tried,
You'd likely go mad from the sheer amount of everything,
Which made a direct look
Down the center of the store impossible.
Whenever I walk into a place like this,
I turn hard to the right, and cling close to the window,
Looking lightly,
Letting in small amounts for my brain to process
Before daring to look up to a nearby floor-to-ceiling shelf.
I need time to digest the heaping shovelfuls of information
My overwhelmed eyes absorb and confound me with.

August 14, 2013
Benson, Vermont

I had originally intended for this idea to be a paragraph of prose in
a novel of some kind, but I didn't know when I'd use it. Instead, I
splattered it into the rough shape of a poem. The first line had
originally read, "It was like walking…" but that didn't make much
sense without more information preceding it, so I altered it slightly.

A Photoriffic Moment

My eyes were dazzled
By the glorious sight of
Rippled orange below
The puffy gray shelf
But only for the rarest,
Faintest half-second
For when I returned
With my camera
Hoping to capture
A photoriffic moment
And found the scene
Faded, muted, unphotogenic
And the colors had shifted
From remember-worthy
To pretty much nothing

August 14, 2013
Benson, Vermont

As I was headed downstairs, I saw an amazing sunset out the back
window. A minute later I had returned with my camera and it was
like something had drained the brilliant and vibrant colors from the
scene. The moral of the story is: don't wait to appreciate the beauty
you see before you.

Lies On The Outside

Who we share our bodies with
Holds a fraction of importance
As the person with whom we choose
To share our innermost thoughts
As the realm of the physical
Lies on the outside
While the deep-seated mental
Lies if it wants to –
But the truth is whispered
Only to the trusted

August 14, 2013
Benson, Vermont

Over the past two days I've read two Cheryl Strayed books, *Wild* and *Tiny Beautiful Things*. This poem was inspired by a mish-mash of thoughts from reading her books.

Pulling A Flock

Not just some wool
Or even a simple sheep
But instead, they're
Pulling a flock over your eyes
And without senses or sight
You're blind to the fact that
Your beliefs and values
Are inconsequential
To the continued workings
Of the universe

August 18, 2013
Benson, Vermont

A few hundred years ago most people thought the Earth was the center of the universe. To publically disagree with this would get you (at the very least) run out of town, tortured, or even put to death by your local religious leaders. It's kind of like it makes no difference to the universe whether or not you believe in gravity or climate change. What you believe will not prevent you from falling off a cliff or seeing your once-lush farmland turn into a dustbowl.

Sidestepping

Walking along a country road
Avoiding the oncoming traffic
Sidestepping the occasional trucks
Speeding up and barreling down
Thundering past in a cloud of dust
Rolling, tumbling, blowing by
Blasting country or classic rock
Fading in the distance behind me
Looking around, I step out of the ditch
Resuming my quiet contemplative walk
Thinking, planning, and dreaming of
Seeing the Sun setting over the Pacific

August 18, 2013
Benson, Vermont

While I've seen it before, I would like this sunsetting mindset to occur on a daily basis.

Poetography

My approach to photography
Is similar to writing poetry
As I'm faced with the scenery
Of underappreciated beauty
I take out my photoing device
Capturing the moment
Preserving the lighting
Hoping to show and convey
The magnificence of what I saw
Framed in the worth
Of a thousand words
Each more progressively descriptive
While impacting the viewer on a deeper level
With my photo-vivid narrative
Hopefully leaving them more enriched
Before they beheld my poetography

August 18, 2013
Benson, Vermont

The other day I realized that my approach to writing poetry is similar to photography. It's like they're the literary and visual equivalents of one other.

Quantum Stitch

Belief past the present
Transcending religion
Adhering to a feeling
Delving deep into the emotive well
Where your gut tells you what's right
And turns out is never ever wrong
Placing faith in the knowledge
That we are more, much more
Than the carbon sacks we inhabit
Where souls are linked beyond lives,
Past the centuries, throughout time
Connected to a source energy
Running through every atom
In every thing
On every planet
In every galaxy
Throughout the Universe
Like a quantum stitch
Holding it all together

August 18, 2013
Benson, Vermont

Over the past few years I have been thinking (and re-thinking) about existence and my place within it. Lately, it seems that everything has been coalescing into a perfectly-meshing All-Encompassing-Theory in my mind. Everything fits. Nothing has ever felt so right.

Our Language's Guarded Mistress

A complexity hardly imagined
Beheld and fermented between
The Amhersty auburn braids
Of our language's guarded mistress
Shrouded in secrecy
Betrayed by blood
Revealed unwillingly
To a world hungry
For the inspiring words
Birthed from the layered passionate thoughts
Of our superhero poetess

August 18, 2013
Benson, Vermont

When Emily Dickinson died, her wishes to her sister, Lavinia, were clear: burn all of her letters. When Vinnie discovered the treasure-trove of Emily's poetry, she went against her sister's request. She did (unfortunately) burn all of the letters that Emily received from other people, but (thankfully) kept her bundles of poems.

Generations Removed

One generation removed:
The center of their world
Two generations removed:
Incrementally disregarded
Three generations removed:
Almost completely forgotten
Four generations removed:
It's like you never existed

August 22, 2013
Benson, Vermont

A Bubbling Cauldron

Most modern poets seem more concerned
With recognition, marketing,
And getting others to talk about their work
Wasting time and words writing promotional copy
Rather than letting their words speak
For themselves and telling their own story –
Inflicting sorrow, like a family full of funerals
Casting shadows, like a mountainous magical conjurer
Directing light, like an adventurer exploring a new land
Inciting sensations, playing you like a beautifully-crafted song
Spurring joy, like the happiness of a purring cat
Or stirring emotions, like a bubbling cauldron
Filled with the thick liquid of deeper understanding
Flavored with a delicious stock of stunning visuals
And seasoned with such a delicate pairing of words,
The distilled textual essence of language,
Which makes it all so easy to swallow
And keeps the reader returning for more

August 31, 2013
Benson, Vermont

In every type of self-created business, creatives are encouraged to find a good balance of making new work while engaging in self-marketing and promotion. I agree with this…except for myself in regards to poetry. I feel that if what one writes is of a solid enough quality, it will naturally find a wider audience. I would rather spend my time steeped in the process of creation than promotion; one is a body of work while the other is merely a billboard.

Don't waste your precious time setting up billboards when you could be creating.

Thell

He will
Tell the hell
They will
Let him
Thell the well

August 31, 2013
Benson, Vermont

While writing "A Bubbling Cauldron", I mistyped and accidentally wrote the word, "Thell." I was intrigued by this word, which, in that instant, seemed to be the bastardized combination of so many words smooshed tightly together in a compact orgy of competing thoughts and meanings. I thought I'd have a little fun and see what I could do with extracting those words into something slightly cohesive.

Before The Little Shower

From my vantage I see
The faded blue-gray
Sun-bleached porch roof
Just outside my window
The light pitter-patter
Asks for my attention
As the sharp tiny points,
Appearing so many at once
Blending, bleeding
Into a solid gray slick
With the rare splotch
Of untouched dry island
Yielding, fading, succumbing
To the barrage from above
Which passes just as quick
As its initial unprovoked attack,
And, over dozens of minutes,
It slowly becomes apparent
That the process reverses itself
Spreading from the top down
And the rare islands, outward
From their unblemished spots
Drying down the slant
Leaving it looking, for a time,
Like an ugly, poorly-done camouflage
But, as with everything, it doesn't last
And soon the roof has returned
Back to the way it was
Before the little shower

August 31, 2013
Benson, Vermont

It's amazing how quickly the roof actually dried. It was wet for maybe half an hour after it stopped raining, and slowly had patches of dryness. Then, ten minutes later, it was completely dry.

Herp Derp

During the fifteen years of my previous professional career
From time to time I dealt with celebrities and famous actors,
Prime ministers, presidential hopefuls, musicians, and governors
And I rarely batted an eye through my bubble of professionalism
Because, hey, they're just regular people with high-profile careers
No big deal, nothing to get too excited about, just doing my job
Then, just last week, I went to see an author give a lecture on writing
And afterward, I ended up having a brief interaction with her –
The quick and steady stream of herp derp that exploded from my mouth
Caught me off-guard; I was horrified by how crazy I must have looked
The several-second scene has replayed countless times in my head
The culmination of each commencing with a mental kick to my mind
For painfully violating my self-imposed celebrity stoicism

August 31, 2013
Benson, Vermont

Last week we went to Bread Loaf to see Cheryl Strayed give a lecture on writing. It was fascinating. I took a ton of notes, was suddenly filled with so many ideas and ways to improve my writing, and was just really inspired. Afterward, Kari got a book signed, and I gave her a copy of *Trying Not To Blink*. That was when I got all herpy derpy. I probably just came across as some kind of fanboy or something, which immediately bothered me on a very deep level because I'm not like that. Ever. So Cheryl, if you're reading this, I'm sorry if I came across like a dork.

Left Handed

Left handed
Right brained
Left leaning
Right hearted
Correct minded

August 31, 2013
Benson, Vermont

Disintegrated The Delineation

The size of things have been put in perspective
The worldly concerns that used to seem gigantic
And monopolized most of my time and energy
Have been rendered insignificant
By the whole-body confirmation
The gut-feeling steadily emanating
From the widely-opened, welcoming heart
As I disintegrated the delineation
And turned my life boundaries into nothing
While expanding the inner "who I am"
Away from how others viewed me
To the one I am meant to be

August 31, 2013
Benson, Vermont

The sense of peace has been welcomingly overwhelming.

The Entire Universe

SEPTEMBER

All That I Do

I'm so very appreciative
For the connection
The closeness I feel
To the Source
Of creativity
That fuels me
And everything –
The vibrational awareness
The comforting envelopment
Reassuring and guiding
Me in all that I do

September 1, 2013
Benson, Vermont

Before this year, I can't really say that "gratitude" has been a word I've used much, or even really given much thought to, but wow, oh wow, have I changed. I can't even begin to describe how amazing my daily expression of gratitude has made me feel.

Upon The Breeze

Upon the breeze is carried
The smoky woody campfirey
Lingerings of a neighbor's fun –
The smell of my youth
An aroma associated
With summer camp
And fall camporees
Memoring beneath the autumn leaves
Crinkling, crisping, crunching,
Underfoot and overhill
Across and throughout
The rolling layered slopes
Set alight by the seasonal fire
A tradition as New Englandy
As the sweetly scented
Steamy escapings
Of the sugar shacks
Making maple syrup
Amid the backdrop of
Winter's recessing grasp
Smells I know I'll miss
On the boundaries of a major city
Portlanded on another coast

September 1, 2013
Benson, Vermont

When I walked the dogs, just now, I could smell the wafting
essence of a campfire hanging in the air. I realized that it was an
aroma I would probably not smell for a long, long time (because
we're moving to Portland, Oregon next month) and it made me a
little sad.

Inspirational Squall

Nestled among foggy hills
Deep within the shaded folds
Of the Green Mountains
Lies a series of yellow buildings
With a creatively-jarring view
A place where the Frost crystalized
Into this transformative place
Where writers do their thing
Under the careful instruction
Of those who came before
Cool air, lush rolling sea-like hills,
Smokey woodstove intaking
With each deeply appreciative breath
Causing the inspirational squall
And the furious flurry of ink rain
On the sleeting sheets of paper
Flying up and out, unto the world

September 2, 2013
Benson, Vermont

Recently we went to Bread Loaf in Ripton, Vermont to hear Cheryl Strayed speak about writing. While waiting for the event to start, I wrote most of this based on what I saw walking from the parking lot to the theater building.

Discordant Motivant

Exercising and needing
An energy boost
Switching on a playlist
Full of heavy, angry songs
Simple and powerful
Dripping with raw energy
And a deeply fuck-you attitude
A discordant motivant
That pushes me up the hills
Speeds me along the straights
Shoves me through the narrows
And helps me complete my run

September 5, 2013
Benson, Vermont

For more of a realistic picture, substitute "walk" for the word "run." When I'm exercising I could be tired to the point of quitting but a really strong song will pop on and I, all of a sudden, get the motivation to push through.

Also, I was surprised to find out that "motivant" isn't a word according to Word. It sure seems like one to me.

Overly Overtly Otherwise

For the past half year
We've kept the gaps ajar
To let in the air
And naturally cool
Out and down the house
But tonight is the first
Since they were flung open
With welcome windows
That we have changed course
And blocked the flow
Since it all changed
From cool to cold
From comfortable
To overly overtly otherwise
And for the next few weeks
We play it by ear
And must be more selective
In regards to the warmth
We now no longer
Want the season to steal

September 5, 2013
Benson, Vermont

Tree Top Teeth

Let your eyes take in the surroundings
From any Vermont vantage or view
And something you're sure to see
Riding the rolling ridges
Of the pervasive mountainous layers
Are the saw-like tree top teeth
Clinging to the sky like a dog consumed
With a defensive tendency for the nature
That changes the curvy gentleness
To something slightly more sinister
When thought about for entirely too long

September 5, 2013
Benson, Vermont

I had the title of this one in my Line Ideas for a week or so, but tonight I wanted to play with it from both the alliterative and visual perspectives. If you squint and tip your head to one side, the poem sorta kinda looks like ragged jagged teeth.

I Can No Longer Comfortably Keep The Moon

I watch the wide moon
Slide across the sliver of my window view
I squint to enhance it
With horizons of light shooting out from the moon's sides
Like a soft peach-colored skyline
Solid at the marble moon-center
And radiantly splayed out at the edges

After a few minutes I have to crane my neck to continue the sight
Due to the Earth's rotation
Like a fancy building-top's rotating restaurant
Trying to constantly give a different view
But in this case I'm confined by narrow boundaries
Between the window frame and the box fan
Until I can no longer comfortably keep the moon
In lined-sight with my appreciative eyes
So I say thank you
And let it continue
On its merry, very early morning, way

> September 5, 2013
> Benson, Vermont

I wrote most of this a week or two ago in the middle of the night when the full moon woke me up and proceeded to slide across my view.

I Want

I want to show the beauty –
Of life, of this world,
I want to give hope and promise –
To the discouragents reading
I want to stir emotions –
Like a debris-churned tornado
I want to make people *feel* –
To know they are truly alive

> September 7, 2013
> Benson, Vermont

"Discouragents" is the best word I've made up in a long while. Definition: people who are negative and discouraged in their daily mannerisms and worldview. These days, it's pretty much everyone.

I would also like to thank Miss Emily Dickinson for being kind enough to gift me a whole bunch of dashes. I promise to use them with reckless abandon.

Hard Luck Exasperates And Fuels The Whippings Of Their Bitter Tongues

The ones with the boisterous voices
Express themselves often
In a manner basically congruent
With their mode of thinking
As hard luck exasperates
And fuels the whippings
Of their bitter tongues
Into a foamy lather
Which coats and sullies
The merest notions of humanity
By the faintest association
As can be roundly achieved
From a simple man
Receiving his phrases
From the talkers in the TV

September 10, 2013
Benson, Vermont

The haunting voice and tone from Neko Case's new album helped inspire this this one.

I See You And I Will Achieve You

Despite being dimly lit in the distance
I am somehow aware of the presence
And am subverting my presentation
In a bid of determined acquisition
For the chance at something whole
Unfettered, unencumbered, and complete
And more inline with what I am destined
As a creative heart deeply beckoned
By the exceptionally interesting interview
I see you and I will achieve you

September 11, 2013
Benson, Vermont

I've been reading Dr. Michael Newton's books about soul stuff
and have been deeply intrigued.

Inhabiting An Awkward Place

I'm inhabiting an awkward place:
Too old to fit the glove of youth
Too young to be taken seriously
Based on my personal demographics
No one will care about my experience
Despite my insight and wisdom
Until I'm old
Or have passed on
And I don't want to wait that long

                September 13, 2013
                Benson, Vermont

Lost

A stirring
Turns into a wave
Thoughts like ghosts
Pass through my mind
Like a breeze in the forest
Making its presence known
In a rejuvenatingly appreciative way
For a single beautifully refreshing moment
Which fades out just as quickly
Left in the rapidly dwindling
Dying motion
Is something unsettled
Leaving a wanting
And because I did not take note
It was soon forgotten
To time and
Lost

September 13, 2013
Benson, Vermont

Several times today I had *WOW!*-level thoughts that I told myself I needed to write down immediately but, because of my locations, each time I told myself, "I'll remember that."

Each time I forgot. I still can't remember what the thoughts I wanted to hold onto were.

Motivational Aspect

There is a motivational aspect
That compels and pushes us
With the act of creation
No matter what form it may take
And when you feel it moving you
Accept and heed its direction
Because great things will happen

September 14, 2013
Benson, Vermont

Trust your gut.

The Envelope Of Charm And Wit

The envelope of charm and wit
Sealed around the personality
With the highest quality paper,
Calligraphy enchantingly beaconed
With an extra special flourish
On the oversized return address
A Charlie Parker postage, plumb level
Illustrating the depth and breadth
Of what could possibly lie inside
Sealed with an entrancingly scented
Flurry of kisses, smoothed out perfect
Sealed with beveled hot-stamped wax
For that unheard of, old-world charm
Sent first-class with return receipt
To not only ensure it was received
But to get the signature of the recipient
Who, despite the window-dressing
Will feel the excitement fleeing
Upon opening the letter and finding
The interior lacking in substance
As every bit of effort went into
Creating the envelope persona

September 14, 2013
Benson, Vermont

See the notes for the next one.

The Envelope Was Tattered And Ripped

The envelope was tattered and ripped
Written and smudged; hastily addressed
The addresser refused to put tongue to glue
Out of some hidden fear they might stick
So it was sealed shut with crinkled clear tape
An ironically chosen "Love" stamp askew
The return address field was left blank
Like the nothingness in the "To" field
As this letter was never intended to return
To the sender or to be delivered anywhere
Except the purgatory of the dead letter office
But somehow, it amazingly managed to make it
From a state of rejection to a more welcoming place
When the one it was cosmically meant for
Opened their mail to find the battered envelope
Ripped through the outer shell and discovered
The most beautifully designed and composed
Letter of eloquence written by an amazing soul
The perfect person who was meant for the recipient
Separated by time and space until the letter's arrival
Which was what restarted their paused happiness

September 14, 2013
Benson, Vermont

Months ago (March-ish?) I wrote down the phrase "The envelope of charm and wit" in my Line Ideas document, and promptly forgot about it. Tonight, I was scrolling down through the pages of unused ideas when I came across it. I started writing about a letter that was beautiful and amazing looking, as if it was describing a very put-together person. That got me thinking about the opposite; a letter where the envelope was all tattered and carelessly addressed by an old lover and tossed into the mail with no address, yet somehow it arrived to the right person, who found the contents to be beautiful and amazing. Since this didn't go with my original intention of "The envelope of charm and wit," I decided to write two poems about the same topic. The previous poem is about a person who is actively pursuing someone and does everything they can to try and impress that person, but when their true nature is revealed, they really have no substance. This is the mirror image to that one.

Rural Expectations Among Men

Walking and seeing
The approaching
Of the inevitable truck
As the driver gets closer
I can now see it happening:
Top half of his palm raised
Up off the steering wheel
With the slightest nod
Of the camo-capped head
To acknowledge my presence
Partially as a manly greeting,
Partially as a way to say
"I've got my eye on you."
In the same shared moment
I mirror his gestures, holding to
Rural expectations among men,
As if to reply, "Hey," and
"Yes, I understand."

September 14, 2013
Benson, Vermont

The Essential Measure

The immortal self
The part that always was
The part that will remain –
Past death, past taxes,
Past everything we know –
Is the essential measure
Of who we really are
Is routinely ignored for,
And in favor of,
The daily things
We choose to busy ourselves with

September 14, 2013
Benson, Vermont

This is something I've been increasingly interested with/focused on as of late.

Equally Unconcerned

Uncertain if I was the other man
Replacing the partner's partner
For an hour of that afternoon
But in the end, it didn't matter
As she was equally unconcerned
With the past behind the person
And instead full-on immersed
With the mutually intense present

September 14, 2013
Benson, Vermont

I was listening to "The Other Man" by Sloan. It's an interesting song because it's from the unpopular point of view of a guy who is the "other man" helping a woman cheat on her partner. It was a neat perspective, so I wrote something based on the song.

From A Factory Of Creativity

The spark of realization
Alighting in my mind
Racing up my pulse
With ideas zipping by
Came from a deeper source
I can rely on each time
A place beyond my current reach
From a factory of creativity
I hope to be able to tour
When I finally arrive there

September 18, 2013
Benson, Vermont

Twice

The randomness of nature
Spoken through a song
Wasn't really random
When the song's subject
So perfectly coincided
With the current happenings
Taking place in my present sphere.
After the first half-measure
I initially skipped the song
But thought the coincidence
Was too striking and hard hitting
So I backed back up a track
To the one chaos had placed
Directly in my audible path
And listened to its message.
Twice.

> September 18, 2013
> Benson, Vermont

I pretty much believe that there are no coincidences, so I pay attention to things like this because I think they're there to teach me something or impress a point upon me.

Shadow Layer

The early morning silhouetted leanings
Once stretched to the western horizon
But receded under the rising star's pressure
Only to diminish to nearly nothing at noon,
Flip around, and reach out to the cooling east
On its way to rejoin the approaching night.
Watch as the last of the lit-portion is pushed
Up the tree by the thickening shadow layer –
One is retiring while the other is growing
And the difference will be darkness

September 21, 2013
Benson, Vermont

I had such a difficult time naming this one. It was either going to
be "Shadow Layer" or "And The Difference Will Be Darkness"
but I wasn't sure which. I went with the former because it was
what I first came up with and, in the end, you really have to trust
your first guess, because that's usually the right one.

(Still not sure if it is or not.)

Never The Same

Life for me has been
Never the same
Ever since a flurry of facts
From over there
Plussed together
With suspicions
From over here
And combined
With assumptions
Conclusions and deductions
From pretty much everywhere
To form the foundational basis
Of my fundamental thinking

September 21, 2013
Benson, Vermont

OCTOBER

Art Is Energy

Art is energy,
Once created,
Then copied
As each copy
Acts newly
And uniquely
With those
Coming into contact
And the initial
Purposeful energy
Is released and affects
The recipient
As it was intended.
The intention
Of sounds,
Of music made,
Is to enchant
Or enrage.
The intention
Of a picture
Or a sculpture
Is to visibly evoke
A particular emotion.
The intention
Of a book
Or a written work
To lead us
On an adventure
Of fictional fun
Or deeper discovery.
No matter the format
Or the chosen conveyance
Art is energy
Building or wrecking;
Inspiring us up
Or dragging us down
With its intentions.

October 1, 2013
Benson, Vermont

I've spent a surprising amount of time lately thinking about the quantum effects of energy as it pertains to art.

Under A Cigarette

The horizon faded
From ripe neon peach
To rusty wash water
In under a cigarette
Leaving the viewer
Missing out on beauty
If they spent that time
Checking their email

October 2, 2013
Benson, Vermont

I was in the backyard with Kari as she smoked, and during that short time the sky went from brilliant perfection to dull and unnoticeable.

A Succinct Summation Of Our Culture Expressed In A Single Simple Thought

Indulging my deeply-rooted cravings
While sitting in a booth by myself
While eating at the local fast-food place
And overhearing the terrifying words
Advice given from one friend to another
Regarding a relationship gone bad:
"You've got to be violent –
 Being right isn't important."
A succinct summation of our culture
Expressed in a single, simple thought

October 3, 2013
Fair Haven, Vermont

WTF? One woman encouraging her friend to get violent and then saying, "Being right isn't important," What is wrong with people?

Let It Go To Weed

A farmer
Clashing and contrasting
With a former lover
And co-land owner
Threatening
In the only way he knows how
By holding up his hands
And saying
He'll let it go to weed
The lack of action
Rippling
Causing reactions
Through curated inaction
Of a scorched-earth policy
Leaving the land
As nature initially intended

> October 4, 2013
> Benson, Vermont

The Geometry Of Middle America

The geometry of Middle America
As seen from the air
Expresses the simple mathematics
Of a region illustrated by
And completely comprised of
Straight lines,
Square right angles,
No wandering,
No meandering,
No need for complex understanding
Point A points directly to point B
Nothing bent, nothing in-between,
No need for needless exploring
Nothing more than pure simplicity

October 6, 2013
Flying from Hartford to Dallas

Hello Plateau

Hello plateau
I see you from up above
In the glinting tack
Cutting the line
Across the sky
Can you see me too?
If so, you're lying on your back
Concerned more with what's above
Than with your weathered neighbors
And the erosional forces
Chipping away at what you are

October 6, 2013
Flying from Dallas to Las Vegas

Rabble Rouser

She got an answer she didn't like
So she talked to someone else
Making up her own policies
For the hotel as she went along
Filling her overexcited mind
With promises never given
In a mid-life desperate grab
For the almighty achievement
Of whatever she can get for free

October 6, 2013
Las Vegas, Nevada

Yikes lady, calm down.

The Light Chasers

A dozen cars
Driving too fast
On a curvy road
None know each other
But all locked together
In the shared quest
To capture the residual
Fearing its demise
They speed up
And blinker right
Into the pull-off
And the light chasers
Hop out, cameras shooting
The daily postcard-quality scene
As the sun's final light
Splashes color on the rocks
The array of sandstone formations
Posing, jutting into the sky
And the shooting continues
Until the day's rays
Are dead and gone

October 7, 2013
Sedona, Arizona

We were totally doing the same thing because, wow, the light and
the scenery was brilliant.

The Hugeness Of It All

Living with excited anticipation
Is wonderful until you're
A moment's breath away
From a life-changing event
When the hugeness of it all
Overwhelms and looms over
As you stand in its cold shadow
And the fear,
The icy-fuck cold fear
Starts to build
While longing and looking back
To the freshly recent past
You're about to leave behind,
The very one you eschewed
For being wrong in some way
But now you want nothing more
Than to turn, run, and cling fiercely
Into its flawed, lacking existence
And embrace its comforting familiarity
As the preferable, desirable alternative
To the dark unexperienced unknown
That is tightly, grasply-held by the future

October 15, 2013
Benson, Vermont

Tomorrow we move from Vermont to Oregon.

Within The Barrel Of It

The looming mountains
Sharper than a chef's knife
Capped with hats of white
Rowed along either side
Of the road that tunneled
Between, lower, and under
The unseen peaks above
And here we are, driving
Like a speed-limited bullet
Within the barrel of it

October 19, 2013
Somewhere in Montana

Montana was unexpectedly beautiful.

Driven A Continent

The comfort of New England
Hudsoned into New York
And the Northeast plained out
Into a Great Plain hatted by
Those equally Great Lakes
Lost behind the blurred miles
As we drove into the past
Where the rivered curves
Laid out by streams and mountains
Ironed out to a uniform plane
Where everything conformed
To the straight lines set by men
For endless days-on-end
Until the majesty of Montana
Peaked up, piqued our interest,
And set things right for a day
With the most glorious sunset
Only for the wonder to be erased
By the nothing of eastern Washington
Until we southerned out
And westerned along
Straddling the curves of the Columbia
Eyes on the mile-wide
Until we were ushered
Into the Hood's view
By the welcoming destination
We had driven a continent to reach

October 20, 2013
Portland, Oregon

NOVEMBER

Kids Need To Feel The Snow

Zooming ahead,
Slowing, landing
The rotors have stopped
The seats have switched
As modes of transport
Have been exchanged
One for another
The oversized truck
Revving to life
The blade lowered
Scraping the road bare
The driver's eyes
Locked on the muted lights
Following in the rearview
Plowing, blasting through
Everything in their path
Unconcerned with the obstacle
Shrugging off the casualties
Robbing, cheating
Those who come after
Of their chance to experience
Driving without a plower
Learning to live and, for once,
Managing life for themselves
Because everyone needs
The hovering to stop
To have the chance
To figure things out
By and for themselves
Just like sometimes
Kids need to feel the snow,
Make their own mistakes,
And figure out solutions
All on their own

November 13, 2013
Portland, Oregon

I read an article on the Boston Globe's website about how "helicopter parents" are becoming more like "snowplow parents" and hobbling their kids' ability to do much of anything in life and it inspired me to write. The title is a direct quote from the article.

In A Semisonic Kind Of Way

The things of the mind
That have been left derelict,
The cravings of the body
That have been left cobwebbed,
The jabbing sticks of pens
That are jutting at awkward angles
Deeply in pockets, reminding,
Awarening of the pile of desires
That have built up over the duration
Needing exploration, needing completion
Needing some sort of satisfaction
But the cards fell without explanation
Causing the blatant cue to be taken
Making the orderly life a horrific mess
Until it settled down into something new
Something wanted, needed, excited,
Settling into something preferable
In a Semisonic kind of way

November 13, 2013
Portland, Oregon

I had a pen (actually two pens) in my pocket that were at a weird
angle and making sitting down at my computer uncomfortable. I
took them out and fired off this bunch of words.

Emergency Brake

Future events, preplanned
By a woman determined
To pull the emergency brake
And put a halt to everything
Currently undergoing
As a way to chase
Dreams of a past life
Lost in another time
To other choices made

November 22, 2013
Portland, Oregon

The Fadeaway

I once had many close friends
Separated by distance
We all wrote often
Updating, apprising, connecting
Then Facebook happened
Which caused the fadeaway
And the falsely perceived closeness
Characterized by being satiated
With infrequent status updates and zero contact
Took the place of the friendships we once had
And left me with nothing more
Than a friend list full of casual acquaintances

November 25, 2013
Portland, Oregon

DECEMBER

Paper Cut Critical

The words were fine
To the casual observer
But...
The tone
Was faintly edged and applied
With just enough pressure
To slice the sensitivity
Like a paper cut critical
Stinging for long hours after
Each of which were peppered
Here and there
With inflicted inflections
Deliberate and intentional
Like salt in the wounds
Meant to cause distress
In that subverted way
That could only be caught
By the one it was meant for:
Me

December 7, 2013
Portland, Oregon

Job Without A But

Midway through life
It would by very nice
To have to a job
Without a but
So when people ask
What it is that I do
I don't tell them
"Well, I do this…"
With a quickly followed
"…*BUT*…"
And have a career
And a source of pay
That I am proud of
Fully once again

December 7, 2013
Portland, Oregon

Late Night Red Light Runners

Sitting at an intersection
At 4:30 in the morning
Before this time zone
Starts its stirring
The light turns green
And I pause an extra two
As the late night red light runners
Have their way
Zipping ripshod
Cutting across the lanes
I should have been between
Resulting in a tragic meeting
Lives perpendicularly ending
In a single mangled point
Cut off to nothingness
By the impatience of a person
Who couldn't be bothered
To wait just a minute
And now they have none.

December 7, 2013
Portland, Oregon

Standing In The Middle Of Her Own Crowd

Ten minutes before the event
There she was
Standing in the middle of her own crowd
Unassuming and blending in,
Unnoticed and surrounded,
Sponging up the energy and anticipation
From the hundreds there just for her
Pretending to be one of them
Staring at the empty stage
While trying to figure the reasons
They came to hear her words
And spending time listening
To the circular swirl of words
Discussing daily life,
Talking about her
And her latest posting,
Or spending time wondering
What TV shows she likes
She absorbs every last word
Until the time comes
And she cuts through the throng,
Stepping into the light,
Turning to face her crowd,
And commanding their attention
With her presence

December 7, 2013
Portland, Oregon

Last month we saw Tavi Gevinson speak at the *Rookie: Year Two* release event in Portland. Before it started, she stood there in the back of the room seemingly soaking up the energy of the room. It was interesting to see.

Re-Mapping

Re-learning
Re-mapping
Re-figuring out
Everything
In a new city
Is a daunting
And an exhilarating
Experience
That is one part
Frustrating
And two parts
Exciting
And completely worth
Recommending

December 7, 2013
Portland, Oregon

I am loving my new city and the daily adventures it brings.

Steeped In Metrics

The weeks have turned to dread as
My day belongs to others
My hours are no longer mine
Every minute is accounted for
Each second steeped in metrics
Measured for adherence
To the company line

December 21, 2013
Portland, Oregon

A life where every moment of every day is captured and measured for adherence to policies is not a life worth living.

Gutty

Held in but bowling out
The gutty, moonlike bowl
Spreading across the equator
Offending the sensibilities
Of the curvy owner
And the dumbed-down dullards
In the immediate vicinity
Effortlessly to create
But takes years to remove
The effort of which
Is akin to mountain moving

December 21, 2013
Portland, Oregon

Red Blinker

Way too early in the morning
When most people are sleeping
I exited the freeway
And found myself behind a truck
Its red blinker signaling directly to me
Methodically, repeatedly, blinking
Showing me their intentions
As the tractor trailer truck
In it for the long haul
Sitting at the intersection
Wanting to continue.
The light flashed
Mesmerized, influenced,
And caused a change of heart;
A change of direction
Making me press down on the blinker
Turning, ignoring what I wanted before
Heading off on new route
Completely unplanned
Happy in knowing
That I'm doing
Something spontaneous,
Something for me,
Something new
Giving me a muchly needed
Well-deserved fresh start
In this old and tiresome position.

December 21, 2013
Portland, Oregon

Seriously. I got all of this from sitting behind a truck at a highway exit while waiting for a light.

The Smell Of Breakfast Cooking

The smell
Of breakfast cooking
Is far louder
And will arouse you
From the deepest slumber
Than any garbage truck
Could possibly be
Even if it rammed your house
And dumped its contents
In your living room
With a honking and hollering
Hit and run
As a phalanx of police
Chased-off in hot pursuit

December 21, 2013
Portland, Oregon

There Is A Privacy To That Side

There is a privacy to that side
A delayed way of thinking
Sheltered by the protective wall
Emplaced through a basic needing
Of separation from the commonalities
Engaged in their rudimentary mores
Thankful for the reflective timing
Needed to contemplate everything

> December 26, 2013
> Portland, Oregon

The house kitty-corner from us is an oddly-designed triplex where two apartments are mirror images of each other, while the third is a repeat of the second. Each section has a garage that sticks out from the front, which in this case, separates that one odd-apartment from the others. When I walked the dogs tonight this struck me in a new way and this poem was the result.

Blasé

Open and forthright
About the kinds of things
That a decade ago
Send me fetal under the sink
Casual and blasé
Discussing the end results
Driving most into foxholes
With bayonets at the ready
But here we are sitting pretty
At a picnic-styled feast
Being all kinds of whatevery
Mulling the conclusionary details
Of what we currently know

December 26, 2013
Portland, Oregon

I Thought I Would

I thought I would
But, you know what?
I don't miss it at all
The season
The snow
The winter drapery
The cold
The sidewalk Slip N' Slide
The trappings found
In this corner of our solar loop
Of traditional New England
I eschewed for milder climes
I thought I would miss it
But you know what?
I don't miss it one bit

December 28, 2013
Portland, Oregon

Comfort In The Songs Gone By

When your life's situation changes
In a dramatic fashion
And you find your friends
Are really more acquaintances
The comfort you seek
And end up receiving
Is most likely found
In the songs that meant the most
Comfort in the songs gone by
The ones that were always there
Ready to help always and forever
And are just a quick click away

        December 28, 2013
        Portland, Oregon

Got Your Back

The most reassuring words
Ever heard in any situation
From back then to forever
Were, "I've got your back."

> December 28, 2013
> Portland, Oregon

Sknow It

To really know the snow
And its nuanced intricacies
Including the various subtypes
And derivatives thereof
Is to be versed enough
To sknow it through experience
And have the ability
To really respect
And appreciate it

December 28, 2013
Portland, Oregon

During the few times it has snowed here, I've been amazed that
people still try to drive all fast and speedy just like normal, and
then become all bent out of shape when they skid off the road.

I Will Succeed

Despite the turbidity
And the churning
Of the swamping water
I have been treading

Despite the brash note
This year has ended on
And those that came before
In the song of 2013

Despite all of it all
That has pushed me down
Sat on me like a bully
And held me there

Despite the dragging
The draining,
The defeating, and
The unforgiving

I will appreciate
I will persevere
I will succeed
Because I am me

>   December 31, 2013
>   Portland, Oregon

Overall, 2013 has been a year full of ups and downs. I am looking forward to things turning around next year.

ACKNOWLEDGEMENTS

I would like to thank the following people for their help and support:

My brother, Todd Nixon who helped edit this collection. Of course I think everything I write is typo-less, but he's the one who finds and corrects those errors. Thank you for making me look slightly more professional.

Kari Chapin, my wife, who is awesome and continues to encourage my writing habit.

My family, Sharon Jandrow, Ron Chapin and Robyn Chapin, who have given a lot of help and support while I wrote.

Finally, and most importantly, *YOU!* I am still always bowled over with amazement when people set aside hours of their time to spend reading my writings. Seriously, thank you. Your continued support is a huge motivator.

IF YOU ENJOYED THIS COLLECTION

Please consider rating it at Amazon.com. As an independent author, having people review my works is critical in helping to increase my exposure and letting new people discover books like this. Thank you!

OTHER BOOKS WRITTEN BY ERIC NIXON

Anything But Dreams: A Poetry Collection

Lost In Thought: A Poetry Collection

Emily Dickinson, Superhero – Vol.1

Trying Not To Blink: A Poetry Collection

FIND ERIC NIXON ONLINE

Website: EricNixon.net
Website: EmilyDickinsonSuperhero.com
Twitter: @EricNixon
Twitter: @EmilyDSuperhero
Facebook: EricNixonAuthor
Facebook: EmilyDickinsonSuperhero
Pinterest: EmilyDSuperhero
My poem, "Riding The Red Line" at The Writer's Almanac:
http://writersalmanac.publicradio.org/index.php?date=2011/08/29

www.ingramcontent.com/pod-product-compliance
Lightning Source LLC
Chambersburg PA
CBHW061817040426
42447CB00012B/2691